A LONG WAY SOUTH

JB

A LONG WAY SOUTH

Salvaged Memories from
Travels in Latin America

SARA STEWART

First published in the UK in November 2024
Journey Books, an imprint of Bradt Travel Guides Ltd
31a High Street, Chesham, Buckinghamshire, HP5 1BW, England
www.bradtguides.com

Text copyright © 2024 Sara Stewart
Edited by Ross Dickinson
Cover design by www.headdesign.co.uk
Layout and typesetting by Ian Spick
Map by David McCutcheon FBCart.S
Production managed by Sue Cooper, Bradt & Jellyfish Print Solutions

ISBN: 9781784779856

British Library Cataloguing in Publication Data
A catalogue record for this book is available from the British Library
Digital conversion by www.dataworks.co.in
Printed in the UK

To find out more about our Journey Books imprint,
visit www.bradtguides.com/journeybooks

Paper used for this product comes from sustainably managed forests, and
recycled and controlled sources.

FOR TANIA, ALEXANDER AND ZOE
WITH MY LOVE AND ADMIRATION.
MAY YOU TRAVEL SAFELY THROUGH LIFE.

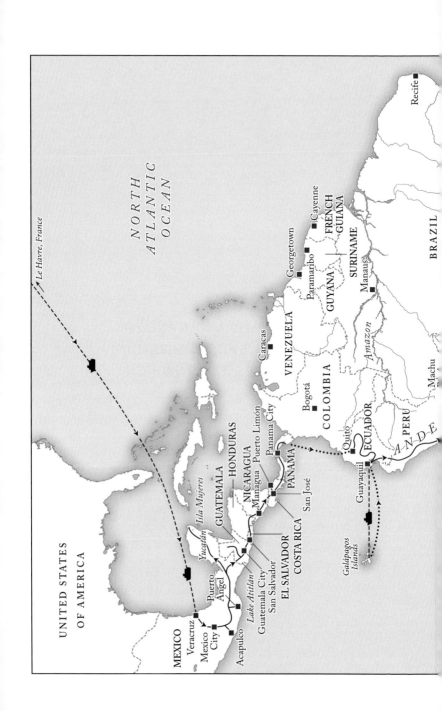

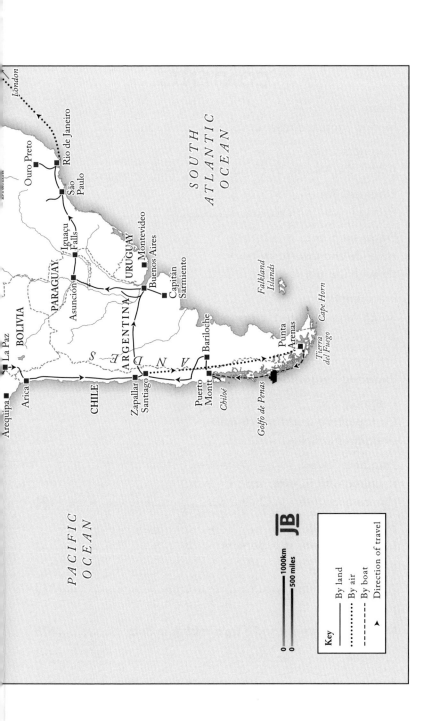

London

Ouro Preto

Rio de Janeiro

São Paulo

Iguaçu Falls

PARAGUAY

Asunción

BOLIVIA

La Paz

Arequipa

Arica

CHILE

Zapallar
Santiago

A N D E S

URUGUAY

Montevideo

Buenos Aires

Capitán Sarmiento

ARGENTINA

Bariloche

Puerto Montt

Chiloé

Golfo de Penas

Punta Arenas

Tierra del Fuego

Cape Horn

Falkland Islands

SOUTH ATLANTIC OCEAN

PACIFIC OCEAN

JB

0 — 1000km
0 — 500 miles

Key
——— By land
·········· By air
- - - - By boat
▲ Direction of travel

CONTENTS

MADRID LIGHTS THE FUSE

Bridge Over Troubled Water

In 1970, aged eighteen, I was offered a place in the Prado School of Picture Restoration in Madrid. Having said goodbye to family and friends I arrived, speaking no Spanish, to find the school had closed due to lack of funding. Determined not to give up and go home, I begged the director to help, and before long was enrolled in the University of Madrid to read fine art. In Spanish. Somehow, I muddled through the first weeks until luck looked after me in the bustling city, and I fell in with a wonderful assortment of glamorous young Spaniards who spoke English better than I did. They introduced me to their families and numerous friends, where there were maids and butlers in white gloves, and large palaces stuffed with dark paintings and heavily gilded furniture.

A political undercurrent rumbled through conversations; General Franco, the now frail, controversial and dictatorial prime minister, was still in power, working out who should succeed him. (Which would eventually be the restoration of monarchy, and a transition back to democracy.) But he could do nothing to detach himself from his legacy of brutal repression.

These were stranger times than I realised, as we danced through the night and breakfasted in small cafés in our evening clothes, along with the milkmen about to start their rounds. Madrid was the city that never slept. I moved into a tiny flat with two wonderful Chilean girls, their long dark hair sleek, their English perfect. Spanish-speaking South American universities had reciprocal arrangements, and Maria Luisa became the sister I'd never had. One day, I promised her, I would find her in Chile, meet her family and see her way of life. Diminutive Pepa, also from Santiago, was studying nursing; one of nine siblings, she was constantly laughing and singing. I relished living amongst them. We had to climb a narrow ladder-like staircase to reach our garret on the sixth floor of the old building, and this breathlessly steep mountaineering tested the hardiest of friends. Before long I had a part-time boyfriend, Toni, the youngest of a large family who welcomed me into their rarefied lives filled with laughter and gossip. Without a backward glance to my previous world, but alive and caught up in my new one, I attended university… sometimes. I worked for a film director, auditioned for television, did voice-overs in film studios, met Charlton Heston and numerous, now long-dead, producers and actors. When I was offered a speaking part in a big-budget movie, I decided instead to accompany a man I was crazy about across the country. What might have been, who knows? The man I obsessed over never noticed, and my chances of stardom vanished.

Faisal, recently graduated from Sandhurst, the British military academy, was an unlikely attaché for Saudi Arabia. A member of the royal family, he was a stocky prince who took me to exclusive restaurants, and ordered wine costing more money than I had ever seen, despite the fact he didn't drink. He was hilarious, with a neat moustache, contagious sense of humour and deep, husky voice. He sat behind his driver, pulling either his left or right ear depending on which way he wanted to turn. Sometimes he flew me down to Marbella for a party, and when I refused to stay the night, ordered his pilot to take me back to Madrid. From him I learned that my left-handed eating was considered deeply offensive to people in the

Arab world, and from then on I began to look over the parapet beyond my European myopia. What work Faisal really did was not discussed. He brought a good-looking American along for a weekend once when we were staying with a bunch of Spaniards in their hunting lodge. Years later I saw the American with his wife and children on a beach in Greece and went up to say hello. He turned on me and growled, 'You have never seen me before. I have never been to Spain.' He knew who I was.

I registered with the British Embassy and it only took a couple of their parties to be included in the general diplomatic orbit. There were copious first secretaries from different embassies, including Christopher Meyer, aka Mr Red Socks, in one of his early postings for the Foreign Office, who later became British ambassador to Washington. He was a partner in crime when Faisal gave me a bag full of money 'as a present to buy a car'. I was always broke, but refused to accept the cash. He was hurt, his genuine kindness had been rebuffed. I was offended. Mr Red Socks brokered a deal, and I didn't get the car, neither did I lose my Saudi admirer. Italians, French, Greeks became good friends as my network widened, and often weekends were filled with pointing a car out of the city and just driving and getting lost. We stayed in tiny villages with hand-stitched linen sheets and gleaming brass bedsteads. We ate from earthenware plates swilling in oil and garlic. There were donkeys in the streets, and all women over a certain age wore black. Life was tough and sparse in the unspoiled countryside, but we swirled in and out in our self-contained, self-centred world.

I reluctantly returned to England when my studies and film work were over, hitching a ride with a charming Englishman whom I had barely known in those two overflowing Madrilenian years. He drove and I map-read while we explored the unknown remoteness of Spain as we headed north. The wide, dusty plains and beautiful, ancient towns gave way to the craggy mountains of the Pyrenees before we rumbled on into France. We shared tiny double beds, clinging to the cliff edges on either side. Innocents abroad. We swam in the sea, were tumbled by strong waves, and stayed in Paris, where the jovial proprietor of our small *pension* brought us breakfast in bed each morning, winking theatrically. We played up to his romantic ideals before heading across the Channel for England.

My chaste English driver was heading to his parents' home, and invited me to spend a week with them in the country. 'I'm afraid you'll have to come on the train with Princess Margaret.'

Thus, I found myself on the platform of Liverpool Street station in the Friday afternoon rush hour. There was a cordon around one carriage, into which I stepped with trepidation. The princess had a reputation for being difficult, for preferring men to women, and being allergic to stupidity. I was tongue-tied and felt immensely stupid, as she sat perched on the banquette, feet dangling above the floor, doing the *Times* crossword. She didn't look up until the train had started. 'What's an impoverished senator earmarked for promotion?' I stared, dry-mouthed, unable to speak. There was nothing to say, I had absolutely no idea. And so the journey continued, it seemed, for months, with her occasionally throwing balls at me which I couldn't possibly pick up.

She had specifically asked for a local couple to come to dinner, to join all the others staying in the house. Fourteen of us sat down, and as soon as she was served, she ate. Fast. She had finished long before the last person had their food, and drummed her fingers on the table. We bolted our delicious dinner: barely finished and on to the next course. She stood up, which necessitated everyone doing the same, and without a word swept out of the room and upstairs. Moments later she called down, 'Have those dreadful people gone yet?' The charming couple whom she had invited slunk away, and the diminutive princess came downstairs again. She played the piano, gave hilarious parodies of the recent state visit by Emperor Hirohito and his family, describing and mimicking how the British royals had no idea the Japanese could speak English, and, as they greeted the visitors on the red carpet at Victoria Station, introduced each other as Lord High Executioner, Yum-Yum, Nanki-Poo and other equally ludicrous characters from *The Mikado*. She was the life and soul into the early hours of the morning.

On my unenthusiastic return to London, I found jobs for three or four months at a time, boring, unrewarding, but they paid my rent and enabled me to put money aside for the journey I was determined to make. I had promised Maria Luisa that I would come and find her in Chile, and despite renewing friendships with those I knew in England, I wanted to see that long ribbon of country for myself, to sit and discuss life with my greatest friend, who just happened to live on the other side of my world. The problem was I couldn't afford to get there.

Uncle John, my mother's brother, whom I adored, was 'in shipping'. He understood the need to explore and leave the shallow pleasantries of everyday life behind. He'd lived for a while in Mexico, and his greatest friend was Antonio Blanco, a shipping magnate with cargo boats steaming between Europe and Mexico. We got to work, searching out every possible contact in Latin America. Friends and parents scrutinised address books, and before long, thanks to Antonio, I had the promise of a free passage to Mexico, and the optimism of several contacts scattered throughout the continent, hopefully still living somewhere 'over there'.

I stabbed at the map, and bought a one-way plane ticket from Rio de Janeiro in Brazil to London, dated a year later. It had long, flimsy pages with red carbon paper, and was my get-out-of-jail card in all countries that required proof of an onward journey. I reckoned, however penniless I was, I could at least somehow make it home.

ACROSS THE ATLANTIC BY CARGO BOAT TO MEXICO

(Sittin' On) The Dock Of The Bay
Sailing

September 1974

As the ferry neared the port of Le Havre, reversing its engines with a roar, foot passengers bunched together to get closer to the disembarkation door. A jostle for the front, and as the ramp crashed down, a race to be off. I stayed on deck a little longer, scanning the hundreds of ships tied alongside the huge misty harbour, hoping to glimpse the cargo boat *Specialist* which was to transport me, along with its load, to Mexico.

The glamorous Mexican owner had stayed true to his offer of a free ride across the Atlantic. There would be no other passengers and I was to pretend to be his niece. Nerves, excitement and apprehension crowded in as I walked down the broad ramp onto the quay and was welcomed by a short, dapper Frenchman wearing a long raincoat and an enormous black moustache. He giggled like Basil Brush, a foxy puppet with his own television programme, gazed up announcing, '*Vous avez les flammes dans les yeux*', and led me to the ship. Ten thousand tons, only three years old and air conditioning throughout. Such luxury. The last of the cargo was being loaded into the hold, sinewy sailors were running over the decks, orders from the bridge rang out. French Basil was agent for the shipping company and invited me to dinner as we weren't sailing until the following day. After all, I was the owner's niece.

But after cross-questioning me about my '*amours*' as we watched cars, machinery and trucks being lowered into the hold, his hands wandered too much for comfort. I declined, and with relief climbed the narrow ramp onto my new home.

I was given the owner's cabin, which had me gasping with delight. An enormous suite of comfortable rooms, luxury I hadn't dreamed existed on a cargo boat. The twinkly-eyed German captain, Heinz Jurgensen, gave me a tour, and as we climbed up ladders and along a maze of pipe-laden passages, we peered into engine rooms, crew's quarters, galleys, the hospital bay, up onto the bridge and down into the bowels. It was a rabbit warren, home to forty men. The officers on board were tall, pale Germans, Ukrainians, Romanians; the crew stocky, short Mexicans and Spaniards, and it took me a while to realise why the officers hurried up ladders ahead of me, while the crew waved me on in front of them with triumphant laughter, so they could see up my skirt.

The rain came down so hard that loading had to stop for the rest of the day, and I sat gazing out of my portholes at the blank canvas outside, intoxicated in the vacuum between leaving a familiar life and waiting on the cusp of the unknown.

Still the rain poured down all the next day, and loading didn't begin again until late in the afternoon. I was shown how to put on a life jacket, where to assemble in an emergency. I shared the captain's table in the dining room and heard the first of many stories about his war, the number of British submarines he had torpedoed. I watched him, a sea dog with chiselled face, not unlike my English naval grandfather. They had fought in their navies on different sides, were responsible for death, and would have found much in common now with their decency and peacetime love of the sea. There the similarities ended. A few days into the voyage I discovered this captain wore a skirt each evening. He crocheted bags and stitched bikinis in his spare time. My grandfather was writing the first ever sea guides to the Mediterranean coasts, sailing for his research all summer, writing in London through the winter months, his books published by John Murray and translated into many languages. I had learned to love the sea with him, and *Denham's Guides*, as they were known, were famous in the yachting world.

But now, we were to sail at three in the morning, and not even the dark cold of that dead time could stem my excitement as I clambered up to the bridge deck, heard the rattle of chains as the anchor was winched up, and watched the tug pull us out, warning red and green lights shining bright to denote port and starboard. As the tug cast us off, a French pilot steered us away from the vast, silent, slumbering ships all around. He took us well out of the harbour before wishing us bon voyage, climbing rapidly down the side on a sheer ladder, jumping into the waiting speedboat and zipping back to land. Walkie-talkies were buzzing, a hive of activity across the decks. We were off.

Calm gave false optimism before violent storms in the Bay of Biscay. The ship rolled and pitched, it plunged as waves crashed over the decks, and I was miserably sick. The first mate, a Mexican I named Cortés, told me the stabilisers were out, but each time I raised my head I had to flop back down, until the captain came into my room and forced me out of bed. 'We are washing ze turbines, so we slow right down. You will be good.' He dragged me up onto the deck, where he tied me to a chair, fed me dry biscuits and assured me I would feel better.

Retching and wretched I sat there, wondering how Nelson managed to cope with his seasickness every time he set sail for another battle. It is a miserable sensation and surprising how many avid sailors suffer from it.

'I have an embarrassing problem on my hands,' said the captain, casting his eyes dubiously around my cabin. 'The steward has been to the officer on duty who went to the first officer who came to me. He is unable to clean your bathroom or make your bed in the morning because of these.' He strode into the tiny bathroom and waltzed back dangling a pair of pink knickers in front of him. 'You see, Jesus, the Spanish steward, is unmarried, and has never had to touch anything like these before. He is humiliated at the thought of having to move them. So in future will you make sure all underclothes are out of sight?'

It was quite clear Captain Heinz was not remotely embarrassed, but relishing his new-found role as matron to the owner's niece.

'Now, 'ave you noticed the Atlantic penis on this ship?' *Der Kapitän* was speaking. 'Come mit me.' I staggered off after him along the length of the deck to the prow, where he told me to look over the edge. Gripping the rail, I leaned far over, too far for comfort, and there was the protuberance just below the waterline. He chuckled and explained that it was known as a Bulbous Bow, which helped water to flow around the hull, reducing drag and therefore increasing speed. This ship was masculine.

Each evening I sat with him at his special table as he made figures of birds from unused paper napkins, while a steward served us enormous helpings of unidentifiable meats, red cabbage and potatoes. Heinz sent tapes to the night nurse and Pekinese with whom he shared shore life.

'I am speaking to my love mit my breast und my belly,' he enthused, insisting I listen to return tapes of his dogs yapping. We solemnly sat round, unable to speak while the din of doggy noises prevailed. Realising this was destined to be a daily occurrence, I persuaded him to lend me his recorder and music tapes. He listed them carefully. Top of the pile was *Take Off Your Dirty Booths*, followed by *I Wear Charlie Shoes*. His misspelling didn't instil confidence in his choices. I wasn't much better off.

Neither could Heinz pronounce his J's, and he tried his best to wear me down with dreary 'foony' yokes of yumping into lakes without a life yacket. But in spite of his often unsavoury, leery remarks, he was a kind man who knew full well I was not the owner's niece.

The officers were keen to practise their English. Tom Schilling aka Baby Face, the engineer, who weighed around sixteen stone and wore figure-hugging powder-blue T-shirts, presumed he spoke it fluently. In a way he did, but it took me a while to decipher 'I screen southand flofeesh' into the thousands of flying fish he wanted to describe. His days consisted of leaning over a rail, shirt off, watching the Mexicans rubbing down the decks; cracked varnish on boards worn with dried salt. Nothing too busy – I could see why he weighed so much.

Days faded into exquisite sunsets as we passed the Azores, changed tack and headed due west. Flaming skies of oranges and reds, wide panoramas of ravishing colours flowing into each other recreated their palettes every evening, while the sun sank below our horizon, celestial reflections staining the sea. Clocks were changed an hour each day as we slipped further from Europe.

Stefan, who had escaped a Romania struggling under its ruthless dictator Nicolae Ceauşescu, was a nervous bundle of fun and extravagant stories. He pointed at shoals of tiny fish leaping out of the water, dolphins dancing in the wash and powering effortlessly in front of us, babies clinging to their backs. Where I had been blind, I learned to see what lay just under the surface. My eyes acclimatised, my legs learned to steady in the swell, and even fried eggs, frankfurters and black pudding sliding around my breakfast plate didn't put me off my stride.

Journal

Climbed up to the bridge deck, and struggled to listen to incoming election results from Britain on Stefan's crackly wireless. At 11pm GMT it seems the Labour Party are in with a three-seat majority, and Harold Wilson is the new prime minister.

Herr Schilling smiled one morning. 'We passed a British naval vessel in the night, so I signalled that we had you on board. They replied how lucky we are!' He was a quiet, shaggy, freckled man who had been all over the world, and hoped one day to settle down and be a pilot on the River Elbe.

He had been woken the previous night by loud shouting, and stomped downstairs to find Skippy the chef and the second engineer tearing into each other. Both drunk, both big men. With blood all over the walls and floor, he'd had to turn the fire extinguisher on them and squirt until they stopped. He injected one of them with a tranquilliser and sewed up a gaping hole at the back of his head. Then the engine broke down and the entire crew started fighting.

'We lost about fifty-seven miles that night.'

I joined the captain on his daily three-kilometre walks backwards and forwards around the decks, listening to more stories of the war, of course from his side. Sometimes a butterfly landed on a lifeboat, occasionally a bird. They must have been lost on their migrations, and I was sad for their aloneness, but marvelled at their stamina. I eventually learned to love leaning over to watch the dolphins way below, until one day Herr Hoffer on the bridge hooted the foghorn which boomed from the speakers around me, and I almost disappeared over the top with fright. The entire deck crew stopped working and laughed hysterically. Laughter eased a kind of tension that was almost imperceptibly building. A woman on board changed the dynamics for everyone.

We had been sailing for ten days. The sun was stronger now, the humid glare harsh, eyes ached, and as we entered the tropics, the wind died. Sunsets expanded across our full horizon, flaming clouds reflected in a blazing sea. If only the seascape artist Turner had been able to come this way.

A gigantic oily swell welcomed us into the Gulf of Mexico, the sky thick and grey as we rolled around in the aftermath of a tropical storm. Going on deck felt like being in a gargantuan damp greenhouse. Gone were the light-hearted jokes with the crew; they knew we were nearing the end of the voyage and were busy painting, hammering, mending, before returning to their quarters to cool off way down below.

The captain made me a money belt and enjoyed testing it for size around my waist. He gave me a five-colour biro, a lighter and skein of string for my travels. As Romanian Stefan remarked, 'That is terrible nice.'

In the dark of night we passed the Bahamas, then as dawn broke we started seeing boats, islands, lighthouses, followed by the horrifying sight of the Florida coast, with a forest of tall concrete skyscrapers stretching along the shore.

With relief we left them behind, until one evening, entranced as always by the setting sun, I noticed pinpoints of light directly ahead of us, still far away, but twinkling over the water. Within moments the decks were throbbing with excitement. Sailors swarmed up to tighten chains and ropes, normally reserved Germans gripped the rails and grinned. Walkie-talkies were in use, as forty men on board anticipated their first night ashore after two weeks crossing the Atlantic Ocean.

Journal

Finished my tapestry – out with the champagne. Stefan danced his Popocatépetl Twist, Tom in terrible state, Herr Mac has the jitters, and Manuel can't even speak. His family is waiting on the quay.

The lights of Veracruz gleamed larger and brighter as we neared the principal port in Mexico, where Cortés had landed in 1519 before the start of his rampage, and where he forced his troops to burn their boats so they couldn't return to Spain. As I pondered my own reaction, I wondered how they must have felt to see land after so long at sea.

The pilot came out in a speedboat, climbed the narrow ladder to board and took us in. A tug pushed. The crew were beside themselves, and as soon as we were securely alongside, no more juddering and rolling, they rushed off to change out of their baggy work clothes before running off into the dark corners of the old town.

At the same moment a swarm of swarthy Indigenous customs and immigration officials appeared on board, making straight for the captain's cabin for their bribe of cigarettes and whisky. No one wanted trouble.

I was sad at the thought of leaving so many men who had become friends, who had discussed their families, their hopes and dreams. This snail was sliding away from its extremely comfortable shell, and part of me wished I could sail on through the oceans, and continue such an easy-going life in perpetual motion. I had read several histories of South America, finished a tapestry, filled a sketchbook, and only now, seeing the shore, did I understand how not seeing land for two weeks had swept away small anxieties, leaving space for introspection.

We arrived on a Friday evening. The customs officials declared they did not work at weekends, so I couldn't leave the ship until Monday. Having carefully packed, I unpacked my bag and watched as Herr Mac sauntered off the ship, smart in white uniform, followed by Baby Face in skintight trousers. I felt like a small child forbidden to join the party, with all but Romanian Stefan gone. He told me how the captain had lined up the officers and crew before I arrived, and ordered them not to touch me, and was in the middle of explaining that the *Specialist* was changing her name to *Rapid Bridge* for the next voyage, when, without knocking, four pockmarked officials trooped into my room and said my bags would be offloaded now, checked, sealed and taken into custody until I departed. I repacked quickly, just in time for the next prying hands to fling everything out again. Satisfied there was no hard porn coming into their country, they signalled no fewer than five harbour porters to take the little red case onto the quay, where it was loaded into a cavernous truck and trundled off out of sight. My worldly goods were gone, but still I had, officially, to remain on board over the weekend.

Not a chance.

Letter to my parents

Veracruz is a small, bustling, gaily shabby town, filled with brightly clad Mexican Indians from all over the country. Backstreet buildings are peeling and dilapidated, but blend into the hustle of flower sellers, hammocks and vegetable stalls. Buses are straight out of Butch Cassidy: ancient, with wooden seats, and windows open to the elements. The Indians wear elaborately embroidered smocks, the whiteness of the linen dazzles, as does the whitewash of the arched colonial houses in the main plaza. There are extreme contrasts between sun and shade, and markets are ablaze with brilliant coloured blooms, jewellery, weavings and fruit. One enters a kaleidoscope of colour. A happy, busy, noisy world after the quiet of the ship.

Journal

Terra firma at last, and it felt odd without the motion of the ship under my feet. Walked into the centre after the day's heat had subsided, and bought Stefan film for his instant Polaroid camera. Passed Skippy, the ill-looking Yugoslav, and engineer Baby Face, joining them for a drink. They said they'd all wished they could have talked more, and got to know me better. Supper of cold meats and cheese on board with the captain, who said I could go and live with him. Touched, but no thank you. Stefan, meant to be on duty watching cargo unloaded, suddenly burst into my room with bananas and cognac, wanting to take photographs. So, as he clicked and poured out his anguish of statelessness along with the brandy, I stood for him, when with a brief knock on the door the ship's agent arrived, asking me to have dinner with him. Stefan hid, I refused the invitation and as soon as he'd left, with a little bow (I'd forgotten I was the owner's niece), Herr Hoffer breezed in to order Stefan back to work.

That evening the Veracruz band was perched on a balcony above the colonnaded houses. They wore immaculate white, stomachs bulging over low-slung belts as they played varieties of instruments, marimbas and drum-like tubes made from turtle shells. Everyone below danced and clapped. No one too geriatric or too young to join in the fun. Smart cadets from the nearby naval college strutted about saluting each other, while old crones cooked delicious pastries over open fires. The officers and crew from the *Specialist* were scattered around town, drinking, dancing, waving as I passed, grinning with optimistic expectation.

Back at the harbour, I watched more of our ship being unloaded. Dockers were hard at work taking off wine, car parts, speedboats and machinery. What a contrast to the Europeans in their drab clothes, dragging crates in the drizzle. These machos were perfect Mexican *bandido* caricatures, with droopy moustaches, brightly coloured bandanas, cummerbunds and baggy breeches. The harder they worked, the louder they sang, as the night filled with sounds and smells. Girls wandered along the cobbled quayside and up the ramps, offering to mend, wash and clean. They wore red lipstick and tight-waisted skirts. Each one a Carmen.

Having no books to read for the next few days, as my case was stashed somewhere in the middle of town, the following morning

I hunted for the bus station. No one I asked gave me the same directions, and no one said they didn't know, which turned out to be a national trait.

When eventually I found my goal, the greasy-haired ticket collector shook his locks and hissed between his teeth.

'Excuse me,' I said in my best Spanish, 'I didn't quite hear what you said.'

'No buses until next week for Mexico City,' came the reply.

FALLING IN LOVE WITH MEXICO

The Most Beautiful Girl
Beautiful Noise

When Cortés was asked what the country looked like, he squashed a piece of parchment in his hand, and released it, saying, 'This is the map of Mexico.' There was no more fitting description of the country as my bus lumbered from the thickly tropical coast around Veracruz up into forested hills, and eventually out onto a barren plateau surrounded by volcanos and snowy mountains.

Letter to my parents

The captain and all the officers lined the gangplank to say goodbye and, as I walked slowly down saying farewell to each of them, I had to force back tears knowing I will probably never see them again. The dockers stopped their work to wave and grin, and the Spanish Mexican crew, bleary-eyed from their nightly escapades, saluted me with brooms and paintbrushes.

The bus cost £1.50 – not bad for six hours. We took a lovely mountain route, keeping off the main road until the end, passing tiny farms and grand estancias. It seems you're never far from extremes of wealth and poverty. The villages are a huddle of shacks, with chickens, pigs and people living under the same roof. Spain is a luxurious memory compared with here. The Indigenous people are small, dark and extremely friendly, different to those on the coast, they paint their homes bright colours and seem to survive on almost nothing.

Travelling through the forests was like going to Segovia over the mountains from Madrid, and I felt as if I was in a Sorolla painting, with deep purple shadows and blinding white sunlight, until suddenly we found ourselves looking down onto the vastness of Mexico City. Because of earthquakes it sprawls, not up, but forever out.

The bus terminal was a whirlpool of humanity flowing in all directions: old men, faces etched like walnuts, carried outsize bundles, babies swung off the backs of strong, sturdy mothers. Buses spewed clouds of black smoke as they revved their ancient engines. Loudspeakers hissed and crackled. I found a telephone kiosk and rang the kind couple who, through friends in England, had offered to have me to stay. 'Hop in a taxi, don't pay too much and head home. Easy.' Away from the din I hailed a battered red car and having put my bag in the boot was about to step in when I remembered to ask how much he would charge.

'Forty pesos.'

'Far too much,' I squawked, horrified, and dragged my luggage from his car.

The next driver said, 'Seventy pesos.'

'Fifty,' said another. 'Very far you know.'

A craggy face grinned at me from the ancient red car as I climbed into it for the second time.

'Honey,' called James, 'come and meet our little guest.' James was English, skinny and charm-free. An avid and knowledgeable collector of pre-Columbian art, he had lived in Latin America all his life. Honey was a Danish Honor Blackman, white-blonde hair, skintight black jeans, shirt always undone several revealing buttons too low. She turned out to be a man-eater. Any man would do as long as he wasn't her husband. She smoked and drank her way through the days, waiting for friends of all nationalities to arrive for dinner, and any man whose wife was away would be led to a private part of the beautiful contemporary house. Sometimes we went on afterwards to chic nightclubs, where we remained until five in the morning while the nymphomaniac danced, groped and consumed a willing target, while James and I sat on the side sipping mojitos, pretending not to notice.

One evening a shiny chauffeur-driven limo came to collect me, and sped to the enormous home, fortified like Fort Knox, of my cargo ship benefactor. The entire Blanco family was there, from matriarchal grandmother to elegant ship-owner Antonio in a suit so sharp you could cut your hands on it. His good-looking sons in their twenties looked louche and sophisticated, while his wife had hair like a helmet and heavily made-up eyes. She was hard to fathom, and it wasn't until much later that I understood her husband had 'many fingers in many tarts', as another Mexican misquoted. Dinner was spectacular: more and more courses were carried into the dining room by a never-ending team of uniformed staff, while I discussed my long-distance travel plans with an aunt adorned with the contents of a diamond mine. We shared the same name, and I gathered she was notorious for suddenly summoning a jet to take her halfway round the world to an opera. But far from dismissing my anticipation of basic bus journeys, she admitted she wished that she too could travel like that, but in her own country it was impossible. She would undoubtedly be a target for kidnappers, and how much she envied my freedom. I had never before thought, for one minute, that being fabulously rich could have any drawbacks.

Dinner over, we climbed high into an observatory to look at the stars, before Antonio and two sons insisted on accompanying me back to my temporary home. But when we reached it, the gates were locked, and no one answered our shouts, bells or car horn. We must have woken up the neighbourhood but not the guard on duty. So, son Enrique, in his slim-fitting expensive suit, began scaling the walls. He got a grip on a pointed railing and hauled himself up, ripping the seat of his trousers into a trailing train of fabric, as he struggled to climb over. But he made it, undid the bolts on the gate and we were through into the grounds, and up the drive. The men scattered round the house ringing bells, banging on doors and windows, until a sleepy maid peered out and let me in.

Although the house, filled with pre-Columbian treasures, was a haven of peace and calm after days spent exploring vibrant Mexico City, it began to feel weird. I had definitely outstayed my welcome. Honey was not amused at the attention I was given by their friends wanting to give me contacts and advice for the rest of my travels, and so I moved into a dilapidated, peeling pink doll's house in the heart of Mexico City, owned by the attractive, eccentric Patrick Tritton. He was Irish, and had arrived in Mexico many years earlier with a pack of hounds and his hunters. He married an exceptionally rich, already thrice-married American, and lived in extravagant drug-fuelled splendour until the marriage failed and he managed to salvage only the Yves Saint Laurent sheets. I slipped into these luxurious remnants of another world, and relished his charm and giggly humour. He was selling the pill to local women, explaining to their incredulity how it worked. And as a result of these intimate conversations, he'd managed to orchestrate a single water tap to neighbouring villages who hadn't spoken to each other for two hundred years. He claimed to be a snake charmer – possible, he said, only if you had never killed one. But I never had the chance to witness his charm offensive on reptiles. He was fully focussed on humans.

Away from the city he owned a run-down estancia near the pyramids, where he still kept ten couples of hounds, and several gleaming horses on which he hunted jackal round the cacti, accompanied by local farmers bouncing around on donkeys. They all wore sombreros, flowing bandanas, high boots.

Letter

There's not even a track to reach his estancia. You just slalom round the huge cactus, past small lakes, and ask a little boy if you're going the right direction.

We arrived in time to see five goats being delivered by Jesus out of the back of a car. Pig, the pet boar, was very overexcited, and Baby, the donkey, chased him through the chickens, causing chaos, while Pig's friend had been castrated, and didn't want to join in the fun. Then there was Cat, who arched his back and arrogantly took no notice of any of us. Paddy greeted us in a billowing red shirt with scarf around his neck, knee boots, gaucho style, Bloody Mary in hand. He is extremely attractive, with wavy fair hair, penetrating eyes and remarkably small feet. Having shown us around the muddle of buildings, hard to tell which were stables, kennels or human habitations, we ate delicious lamb, wrapped in rosemary, from the farm, cooked over an open fire, followed by a siesta, where we lay back on a mound of cushions while he smoked something strong and sweet-smelling. It was dusk by the time he insisted we walk to a ravine to see his favourite White Owl, but we couldn't find her. On our drive back to the city, we passed a car crash, and a dead man lying in a heap on the road.

The week before Paddy's friend had driven me to the ranch in his clapped-out VW, the neighbouring landowner was kidnapped by precisely 176 men. Although I never discovered what happened to the hapless man, I like to think that his family paid the ransom, it was split amongst neighbouring villages, that equilibrium and peace were restored, until the next time they ran out of money. Paddy was a chain-smoking magnet for near disasters, which he relished exaggerating into tidal waves of hilarious stories.

I explored the vibrant, seductive country on local buses, which looked as if they had been requisitioned out of a 1920s movie, as they stopped to pick up anyone waiting with chickens and milk churns by the side of the road. The passengers were constantly laughing and chattering to me, or simply staring in astonishment. Sometimes they'd heard of England, more often not, but as long as I wasn't American, a gringo, all was well. Rumbling along, verges were a riot of wild orchids and gladioli; raucous birdsong competed with excited children selling iguanas whenever we came to a halt.

Amongst the obsessive sightseeing of ancient ruins, higgledy-piggledy cobbled towns, churches rich with gold, incense and the weight of Catholicism, I stayed with generous contacts, meeting artists, musicians, academics.

A weird Scottish trompe l'œil painter in San Miguel de Allende, with whom I spent a few days, belied his thirty years. He was entirely Victorian, caught up in a haze of Dickens and the Brontë sisters, left to dream in his make-believe world, with an idiosyncratic resident priest for company. The town was a multi-faceted rainbow of colour, of high-walled houses hiding talented Mexicans and a mixed bag of foreigners. Sylvia, a strained-looking Englishwoman, also kind enough to have me to stay, banged on about her ailments. She had a disease in her vagina. She had scars on her stomach. Her exceedingly dull husband spoke pedantically and pompously about the life he used to have, and whistled if a moment's silence muscled its way into his soliloquy.

It was a bizarre place where almost every other foreigner was American. They packed the little squares all evening greeting each other with delight. I met Garry who worked for *National Geographic* and told me stories of vanishing tribes in the jungles of Mexico, of brutal missionaries. I drank thirst-quenching, freshly squeezed *limonada preparada* with bearded architect Freddie, visited Dan whose paintings reminded me of Gauguin, his deep voice out of kilter with a skinny frame. He inspired me to sketch from the terrace where I was staying, out of whistling range. But it felt odd to be surrounded by so many Americans, and I became desperate to extract myself from the gringo web of gossip, and hit the road.

For the first time in a month, I needed to find somewhere on my own to stay. My guidebook recommended the Hotel Senorial in Morelia as 'clean, comfortable and full of flowers'. It was squalid and smelly, but a plate of chicken and beans was edible, and I was happy to be by myself once more.

In enchanting Pátzcuaro, the market stretched down to the shore of a vast lake where Indigenous locals paddled dugout canoes, fished with monster butterfly nets, and in their gaily embroidered clothes, babies on backs, they brought their spoils ashore.

Letter

Eventually I had to leave Pátzcuaro, and had a final wander around the town and vibrant market, coming across an old girl who must have been in her nineties wearing brightly coloured clothes, trying to heave enormous blocks of wood into a church cloister. I went to help her, and she burst into giggles saying she felt she was dancing with a very clumsy partner. She looked exactly like that, roaring with laughter in her long skirts. Everyone is so friendly and such a contrast to the sullen, suspicious old crows in Spain.

Food played a colourful and important part of each day. I cruised market stalls piled high with bright exotic fruits, choosing what to buy to divert and sustain me on yet another long bus ride. Often an enormous avocado, bread, cheese and an unknown fruit, bartered with women wearing embroidered smocks as they presided over baskets of vegetables. Street food was spicy, endlessly mouth-watering, with combinations of flavours I had never encountered. I crunched ants, tiny fish still wriggling as they were dropped into boiling oil, tortillas with melting cheese dripping onto my already grubby clothes, chicken in bitter chocolate sauce. As the Day of the Dead loomed, gravestones were laden with food, and cemeteries took on the appearance of profligate picnics. Mexicans were fatalistic about death. If a child under a year old died, they believed it became an angel; someone with intellectual disabilities was a *niño de Dios*, a child of God, and treated with great care and respect. Most girls I saw over the age of about fifteen were pregnant, many having no idea where babies came from.

Picture-postcard sunsets washed pink stone houses and majestic colonial buildings with veils of gold in every new town I explored.

They shone like precious jewels as the air filled with music from local mariachi bands striking up for the evening, leaving me giddy with such an opulent sensory overload.

My crumpled clothes stuck to the broken plastic seat on an overcrowded bus to Acapulco as we creaked for seven hours through mountains, past squalid villages, dry riverbeds, lame donkeys and beautiful scenery. The police stopped us, ordered us all out, and roughly searched bags and bodies for drugs and guns. Then we broke down, and a madman on board started screaming with fear as afternoon turned to dusk. Stories were rife of the dangers of driving this route: babies were said to be thrown across the road into the path of an oncoming vehicle, and as the horrified driver stopped, he and his passengers would be murdered, bodies and belongings never seen again. But eventually, miraculously, our driver somehow managed to get the bus going, and it was with exhausted relief that we creaked into the once great port of Acapulco.

The first three hotels took one look and told me they were full. There wasn't a soul in sight, but I was puce in the face with the sweltering heat, the air at sea level weighing heavily.

The town was a fragment of its former glory, but bougainvillea-covered houses had unspoilt views over rocky bays to the Pacific Ocean, flowers tumbling in profusion from every crevice they could find. It was a tropical paradise, and I grew to love the place tinged with danger, and incurious occupants. Each evening local men of all ages stood on narrow cliff ledges both sides of a shallow, tapering bay. Barefoot, they climbed up the sharp rocks, crossed themselves in front of a small altar, and as the waves rolled in they dived, but if they misjudged the wave and it was on its way out, that was the end of a wretched life. They earned meagre coins for such dangerous work, watched by a few American tourists who seemed unaware of the potential danger. I was told the divers who survived went blind quite young from the pressure, although the pressure of poverty must have been equally intense.

The manager of the hotel which had eventually deigned to allow me to stay announced he wanted to take photographs of me to use as postcards. If I agreed, I could stay on for free. So, cheapskate that I was, I draped my pallid bikini-clad body around the pool, under no illusion that I would help entice more punters, while Miguel snapped his box Brownie camera furiously and unprofessionally. I was taken waterskiing, but the boat was like an old armchair and pulled me up so slowly that I fell over, hit my nose on the ski and watched in horror as blood poured down my face, turning the sea around sludgy red. All I could think of were the sharks that must surely be torpedoing up the coast to find me.

It was time to drag myself out of my torpor, and move on to explore less-travelled parts of Mexico's dramatic coast.

Roads were dirt tracks, filling each bus with thick dust that choked us all. We stopped at the top of a steep hill in the village famous for its magic mushrooms, where several passengers climbed out clutching empty sacks, ready to fill them with the staple of their impoverished lives, and help ward off the pain of their mental and physical infirmities.

I stayed in small fishing villages, roofless huts under starry skies, washing myself in the sea, where vast manta rays floated above the waves, or hosing myself down with water from the roof at the back of a shack. Giant frogs crept out of the gutters, and friendly fishermen paid for my drinks at shacks on the beach. Every evening loud music from a jukebox pumped out from Pepe's tavern, while day and night the Pacific pounded onto the sand, a powerful reminder of its strength and unpredictability.

Along the coast I met educated Mexican runaways who had left city life and made stunning homes on islands and remote bays out of local materials, with sand as their floor, leaves their roof and hammocks their bed. They had gone native with long hair, bare feet and a penchant for magic mushrooms. Time seemed suspended for them in a haze of smoke and sunshine, and drugs. I had an introduction to one of them, Eugenio, who had left a successful interior design company behind in Mexico City, along with high-profile clients, and now lived far from any inhabitants in a large shack along the coast. A beautiful young local named Regulo, his dark hair bleached by the sun, flawless white teeth and a perfect body, looked after him, driving the narrow longboat to collect supplies, spearing fish as he swam naked, effortlessly, underwater. He picked me up one morning, shell necklace around his neck, with a cool smile that told me he knew he was beautiful, that he was privy to the private life of high-flying aristocracy. I was welcome to join for a day or two, but would never have access to their inner sanctum. I wished I could stay on longer, high on the sound of pummelling Pacific waves that distorted reflections of the most beautiful sunsets. Along with the giant manta rays there were terrifying long sea snakes, playful dolphins and gentle turtles. Shells designed with incredible complexity decorated deserted beaches, and along with Regulo, who looked after me with solemn consideration, new-found friends dived for lobsters to cook over fires in the sand. At night, as the stars came out, glowing phosphorescence illuminated the ocean.

One night in tiny Puerto Ángel, a village of twenty houses, a commotion woke me and I rolled out of my trestle wooden cot to look down over the wall of my roof-free room. There were dozens of men fighting, shots fired, a man lying as if dead. Before long a battalion of police arrived from the local garrison and rounded everyone up, marched them off, women screaming. The wounded were loaded onto the back of the fish truck, and the dead man was only dead drunk. It was like a rehearsal for a Gilbert and Sullivan opera, but even paradise had its undercurrents.

It was hard to say goodbye to Regulo. As days passed sitting on the beach in a haze of smoke from hand-rolled joints, amongst a bunch of Mexican dropouts, he made sure I was protected, walking me back at night to my room with no roof, views open to the sea and sky. A beautiful apparition, he arrived quietly each morning to check all was well, understanding how drink, drugs and boredom can distort the most benign of us. When the time came, he carried my red case to the bus stand, waiting with me as tears trickled down my face.

Laboriously, buses picked me up and dumped me down, as I made my way across Mexico to the Yucatán Peninsula on the other side of the country. Weeks amongst the fabulous ancient Mayan ruins were punctuated by dense steamy jungle, houses built of straw, delicious local food, and an eternal hunt for somewhere cheap to stay. I was managing to live off about £1 a day, which somehow covered everything.

Letter

The old rattletrap bus dumped me, rather like the Lone Ranger without a horse, in the middle of nowhere. Far in the distance was a tiny village, which, with its one main street about three hundred yards long, was Palenque. I struggled with my case – now mended with string from a sack of grain, generously given and knotted by a farmer, plus a length of spare fabric that a fellow passenger pulled from his wife's bag – and slowly passed the bar, horses tied up outside, silent under the weight of their heavy saddles, men lounging on the verandah in sombreros. Real cowboy country, where everyone rides around on horses or donkeys, and cars are a rarity. I came across two girls on the side of the road and asked them where the little hotel was. They giggled at each other, and I realised they couldn't speak Spanish. They were pure Mayan and, as I now know, most of the locals speak only their own dialect, not even the same one as the neighbouring village. They are sing-song languages, lovely to listen to. Women wear brightly embroidered smocks, their hair in pigtails, no shoes. They seem always to be pregnant and carry everything on their heads wrapped in shawls. And, as ever, they are friendly, laughing and chattering, even if they know I can't understand a word.

Each home has a resident cockerel, which all seem to be in a different time zone from reality, consistently crowing through the night, which means I feel I'm sleepwalking through the day in a constant daze.

A local bus crowded with field workers splutters to the fabulous Mayan ruins nearby. The men use sword-like machetes, which they carry from a belt in beautifully crafted leather cases, with which they slash crops, trees, grass, anything that needs cutting. When they widen a road you see groups of men hacking back the undergrowth, and treading down the earth with their bare feet.

The ruins feel as if they belong to another world, so many different pyramids, temples and far more to be excavated, set in deep jungle, totally un-touristy and unspoilt. I spent all day wandering and watching as pools of sunlight glinted through the tangle of branches, spotlighting birds and insects, throwing shadows, as I studied history books, trying to understand.

More faltering buses through the Yucatán dropped me off on the side of the road to scramble along overgrown tracks past rivers and waterfalls to ever-more-impressive ruins. My knees ached from climbing the steep, narrow steps of Uxmal, of Chichén Itzá, and my eyes smarted from squinting into the strong sunlight to relish spectacular views from their peaks.

Along the picture-perfect coast, with white sand, islands and turquoise sea, lanky fishermen cooked delicious freshly caught delicacies on the beach, where they lived in hammocks slung between palm trees and scratched a meagre living.

I arranged to accompany one of the men on his boat for a day of fishing and swimming. It never crossed my mind Luis might have ulterior motives beyond showing the small neighbouring island to a stranger, in exchange for a few pesos. As we chugged across to Isla Mujeres, he explained how he caught fish with just a simple line and lure. Shoals of small barracuda wriggled around, and as the day rolled on and the sun sank low, I asked to be taken back to where we'd started. He had other ideas, and tied the boat to a rickety jetty, indicating I should follow him to the local bar. There was no one else around, and I kept my distance as we walked over dunes, until a run-down shack with broken railings came into view. There was music playing, several men smoking and drinking glanced up and took no notice. I felt I was in a movie, and any moment the director would arrive and tell the crew to wrap it up for the day and all go home. But no one arrived, and it was dark. I asked Luis again how

I could get off the island, and one of the guys drinking indicated his motorbike, and said he'd take me to the ferry. Naive or what? I climbed onto the back, and off we roared into the dunes, where he stopped, gazed up at the moon, thought better of any other ideas, and skidded on to the harbour, where he left me to sit on a broken metal bench for the rest of the night.

As dawn broke, a noisy little ferry took me off the tiny, sparsely inhabited island, and a beaten-up bus, which broke down five times in the heat of the day, arrived finally at Mérida station. The pigs and chickens were as disgruntled as the rest of us, and a forty-three-hour stop-start train ride on a slatted wooden bench brought me back, filthy and exhausted, the only foreigner amongst the crowd, for the final time to Mexico City.

As I dragged my case up the narrow stairs of the familiar pink house, I heard voices and realised Patrick must be having a party. High altitude combined with December cold; his house was like a block of ice. Tim, the stuttering Mexican valet who would have won an award as a character from *Fawlty Towers*, beckoned me into the sitting room where, to my amazement, sat Shipping Uncle John and his beautiful wife. They were elegant and cool, had called in for a drink, unaware that I had even met Patrick. I was beyond dirty, my teeth furry, and barely greeted them in an embarrassed bid to go and wash. Not so easy – to reach the bathroom you had to go through a squalid, ant-infested kitchen, and then out across the roof. After ages searching for a bathroom light switch, Tim told me there wasn't one. I had to, 'T-t-t-t-turn the bulb in the ceiling in its socket.'

I loved staying in this crazy place. Patrick gave eccentric parties for transgender people and cross-dressers, for actors, and grand

Mexicans with women who weren't their wives, while Stuttering Tim had regular orgies in the bath, after which he slept on the floor with a blanket over his head.

The man who had just produced and directed Liza Minnelli in *Acapulco* took me to dinner and told me stories of Sharon Tate, whom he'd seen two days before her murder. Diego, who called himself Brigitte, was a scraggy Danny La Rue, with outsize false eyelashes that fluttered like butterflies, and a shiny green frock that shimmered like a fly's wings. I had never encountered such a variety of talented creative people, and was addicted to the excitement of it all. Night after night I was shown new corners of Mexico City, throbbing with music and colour, high on mescal, dancing in the streets, hundreds of bands.

One afternoon a woman in the museum hurried through galleries telling us to leave immediately. Outside, streets were filling up with people pouring out of offices, hotels, shops. Chefs and waiters crowded the narrow lanes, men in the clothes of their trade stood looking anxious, women were crying. Cars had stopped. Then it started: the lamp posts began swaying, then the traffic lights. I looked up at the tall buildings all around, and was frightened that they might tumble on top of us. The ground was unsteady. It was like being back on a boat. Several people screamed – they had probably been caught before in other more severe earthquakes, and this sudden frightening episode brought the trauma straight back. The world seemed to be swaying a long time, but when it stopped, people yelled at each other to get away from the buildings before the aftershocks started. I learned later the epicentre was over a hundred miles away, but it was scary, and the realisation that everything deemed static could crash around us stayed with me a long while.

I met Fernando and fell deeply, passionately in love. He was tall, languid and artistically pale, an intense and perceptive scriptwriting director who turned my mind inside out. I became jumpy and jittery with the thrill and uncertainty of life.

'Cancel your dinner tonight,' he would say.

'I can't. I have a conscience.'

'Maybe, but you don't have a contract.'

He lived life by his ideals, and a part of me felt I should leave this perfection intact and never see him again.

'This,' he said, pulling out his 'F' key ring, 'does not stand for freckles or flat feet, but for fickle-fingered fate. Why are you leaving?'

'I must move on,' I replied.

'There's no such word as must. This is your life. Must doesn't come into it'. He opened my eyes a little wider, and scrambled my brains.

As we had dinner with his business partner Raul, who had given Jaqueline Bisset her first role, Fernando gazed at me, saying, 'You're like Shirley Temple, forever young. When you leave me, listen to Charlie Rich singing "Hey, did you happen to see the most beautiful girl in the world". Listen to the words.'

I listened, and I cried.

My visa for Guatemala was running perilously close to expiring, so with deep sadness, and an extraordinary number of friends who came to wave me off, I squashed into an overnight bus for Oaxaca, where I had already spent days exploring the lively markets and spiritually powerful Zapotec ruins in the hilly countryside around. I had made good Mexican friends there, especially the handsome Mayan, Guillermo – photographer, film producer, inspiring anthropologist – who owned a gallery already on the international radar, and counted Marlon Brando amongst his friends. He had taken me under his wing, driven me to hidden ruins in the hills, introduced me to his family and friends. But this time it was simply to change buses, and so, after eight hours of grinding gears and squawking chickens, I clambered onto the next boneshaker with a spare seat, and rattled off towards the Guatemalan border. I had lived a short, complete life in Mexico. It hurt to leave.

Letter

In the early hours of the morning we shuddered to a stop in San Cristóbal, still very much in Mexico, an ancient cobbled village set in beautiful hills. The mist was thick and dead cold, but before long I was sitting at a large kitchen table belonging to Dona Maria, where I wolfed down a huge bowl of scrambled eggs and beans, scalding coffee and biscuits, for about 15p. Her young children washed the dishes, laughing and chattering as they sprayed each other with soapy water, while parrots flew around the huge trees outside. The market is one of the most primitive and colourful in all Mexico. Locals come in, barefoot, from their villages in the hills, wearing distinctive handwoven tribal clothes, usually black with red bands. Men dress in shift-like serapes with cummerbunds; women in big skirts and tight embroidered jackets.

None of them speak any Spanish, but it's fascinating listening to their different dialects. Stalls are laden with herbal medicines claiming cures for any ailment you could dream of.

I went to find a ranch belonging to Americans whose names I'd been given, and who had invited me to stay. Passing through huge fields full of horses I eventually reached the house, out of which appeared a rather scatty old couple. He must have had a stroke as he was slow and vacant. She was tearing round in circles, so I made excuses and fled.

The next bus I caught lumbered straight to the Guatemalan border. After almost three incredible months the moment had really arrived. I was actually leaving, shedding all the friends I had made, the country I had fallen head over heels in love with, folding memories in with my luggage. These I could unpack along the way and hold tight.

Fickle-fingered fate rolled her dice, and I never did see Fernando again.

HIGH LIFE AND LOW LIFE BY BUS THROUGH CENTRAL AMERICA

Guatemala

Your Song

After drinking brandy that burnt my throat, from a new-found travelling friend's flask, I slept deeply for my final night in Mexico. At five in the still-dark morning, rolling reluctantly out of an uncomfortable tin bed into the freezing air of Chiapas, I dragged my bag to the bus terminal, breath steaming clouds of vapour into the clear, cold, predawn day.

Heading for the Guatemalan border, the grinning driver waved at everyone we passed as we cronked through hills, thick with tree-covered lush vegetation, palm houses and Indigenous locals walking barefoot on the stone-cold soil.   We stopped for a breakfast of restorative, scalding scrambled eggs and beans in a dirt-floored shack, while the sun rose, flooding a cloak of colour over the countryside. As the bus headed closer to the border I felt as if I had landed in the middle of an exquisitely illustrated book of fairy tales: the landscape became more impossibly beautiful. Wildflowers created mantles of yellow and pink, white lilies grew in profusion, branches were bent with blossom and others with fruit. It was a magical land of plenty, with no outward sense of the political tensions about which I had heard so much.

Guatemala had been struggling with civil war since the early 1960s, with discord between the government and many Indigenous left-wing groups. Now, in the 70s, Mayans had begun demanding greater equality, protesting against forced labour and the pressure of Christianity. (1982–83 was to be the bloodiest period in Guatemala's history, when the government initiated a campaign to wipe out the country's Indigenous population, and an estimated seventy thousand were killed.)

Several impromptu passport checks momentarily stopped us, until we reached the point where politicians had drawn arbitrary lines across maps, and Mexico came to an abrupt end: a couple of wooden barriers and a few huts. The lounging customs men leered at me, unpacked everything I possessed and laughed together as they chucked it all out onto the rough board that doubled as their desk and dining table. But as I was almost the only foreigner, it wasn't long before the whole lot was bundled back into my bag, the heavy stamp inked and thumped down into my passport. I was waved through with a flourish.

It took a while to find another vintage bus, to load my case onto its roof and wait for it to take me on my way. This time the driver pressed his thick fingers firmly on the horn. It sounded as if a rusty nail was scratching a metal barrel, as if each gasping rasp was its final breath. Every leg of the journey created its own tune that set it apart from the previous one. Mexicans and Guatemalans climbed on and off at seemingly random stops, as I watched and wondered what stories their lives held.

Letter

Guatemala is like a fairy tale. It reminds me in some ways of inland Yugoslavia, although it's more compact. Everyone has told me how beautiful it is, but I had never imagined anywhere could be quite so perfect. It is the brightest green you can imagine, with bubbling streams of clear water; every hill is decorated with patchwork-quilt fields, and roads corkscrew their way through the mountains. Hairpin bends are scarily steep as they tip us through cool pine forests, and on down into rolling hills.

Warm sun and cool air, it's like a hot spring day in England. Ninety per cent of the population is Indigenous, speaking no Spanish, weaving their own cloth – as in Chiapas, although they look different to the Mexicans. The women carry baskets and water pots on their heads, wear the gayest colours, with skirts down to the ground, and often funny hats that are just brims, with no base. The children are adorable, dressed as miniature versions of their parents, while the men look terrific in thick cotton shift-like tunics, which come down to their knees like a dress, with a wide cummerbund round their waists, and either bare legs or heavily embroidered stripy trousers, cut off at the knee. A kind of exotic pair of Bermuda shorts. Each person in their tribe or village wears identical clothes, dependent on local dyes and fabrics. It's fascinating watching them, just as they find it riveting to stare at me.

I climbed off the bus, literally in the middle of nowhere, and sat on the grass beside a herd of goats watched over by a woman weaving on a small loom. I tried to talk to her, but she didn't understand, and wasn't interested anyway, but we sat in companionable silence until a local minibus came by and scooped me up, on its way down to Lake Atitlán, the deepest lake in Central America.

We dropped two thousand feet in half a mile as we careered round the steepest bends, and I clung to the seat in front trying not to lurch into an exotically dressed woman next to me, with a baby asleep on her lap. She had flowers in her black plaited hair, and small gold hoop earrings. An elderly man my other side had his hat pulled over his face as he slept, seemingly undisturbed by me crashing into him as we twisted and shook our way down.

I can understand why some people call this lake the most beautiful in the world. Steeply cultivated hills and forested volcanos march straight down to the water's edge. It's vast, with only a few small Indian villages clustered around. The sun was setting behind the mountains as we arrived, transforming the lake into a misty pink dream. Hard to put into words what a mythical land this is.

I spotted a couple of travellers at Panajachel's small terminal, waiting for their bags to be pulled out of the bowels of an ancient bus, and, assuming with their tanned skin they were Mexican, went to ask them in Spanish if they knew anywhere to stay. Beryl laughed at me and said, with a very slight twang in her English, 'I'm South African, and Garry's from Canada.' Thus began a lifelong friendship which lasts – as I write now, fifty years later – to this day. They were travelling the world for three years, renting small apartments wherever they stopped. Both were enthusiastic cooks, delighted with the markets, creating experimental dishes of new vegetables, leaves, fruit and fish. Only the meat, strung up, possibly for several days, looked dubious. Chickens squawked in small cages before being extracted; necks wrung, and feet tied, they were tossed into a bag. Barry and Geryl, as everyone muddled them, were adorable to me, and offered to keep my bags in their small apartment so that I could rent a tiny room somewhere nearby. We met each evening for drinks and delicious dinners cooked by them on a single gas ring. Beryl had been kicked out of South Africa as a student for her anti-apartheid views. She had an infectious high-pitched laugh, and bore with equanimity the deep pain of an early hysterectomy. Garry had jumped off a naval ship years before in Vietnam, and was resident of nowhere. He played the guitar, long blonde hair framing a handsome face as he sang. A picture-perfect hippy.

Each morning I slipped out of my narrow bed at sunrise, as mist rose off the water, to sit on the wooden jetty and watch Indigenous locals and their children in dugout canoes paddling ashore for market.

Across the lake it was wash day in the scruffy village of Santiago, and it seemed every woman had gathered at the water's edge to wash her clothes. They sang and chatted as they beat skirts on stones, and schlepped embroidered shirts in and out of the soap-cloudy water. Some carried heavy pots on their heads as they walked briskly along rough tracks to flimsy homes. Wearing long skirts they simply stopped to pee where they were standing. Sewage seeped down slopes forming rivulets in the dirt. In the little tin Jehovah's Witness church, men sat on one side, women and children on the other, in their best brightly embroidered clothes, chanting in Mayan. Neatly stitched embroidery was almost always red. The so-called Catholic church was thick with incense, adapted to local beliefs, surrounded by the tiny market, where several women squatted round baskets containing maybe three eggs, or a couple of avocados. Occasionally a skeletal, pecked chicken peered anxiously over the edge, as if it knew it would never make it to the other side of the road. I was touched, almost everyone I walked past laughed and waved at me, grinning and beckoning.

After a blissful hot shower in Garry and Beryl's small home, the first since Mexico City, I felt newborn, energised and happy, as

I listened to their stories of life on the road. They were generous, contagiously free-spirited, and it was tempting to stay on in this Eden, but being British I had only been granted a ten-day visa. British Honduras, which bordered Guatemala to the north, had recently changed its name to Belize, and was the last British colony in the Americas, a connection furiously disputed by the Guatemalans. So, after a final dawn over the lake, I prised myself away from the safety net of friendship and found an overcrowded bus bound for Guatemala City. As we lumbered up twisting roads into forests where I had walked, following narrow tracks, listening to quetzals and woodpeckers chirping and tapping, I took a last look back on to the deep, dark lake, ringed with volcanos in the misty distance, while all around were hairpin bends and gorges interlaced with fields of flowers.

The capital's terminal was chaotic. It looked like the graveyard of all derelict buses on this side of the Atlantic, swamped by the main market. Baskets filled with tomatoes sat on colour-coordinated rusty red bonnets, vast branches of bananas leant against windows, people stretched out in the shade of their unpredictable transport, and yet, astonishingly, an engine would stutter into action, chickens squawked and fled, baskets tumbled into the dust, and an antique behemoth would grind slowly forwards, or reverse into a pile of oranges amidst clouds of diesel fumes.

I boarded bus number seventeen, its numerals at a jaunty angle behind yellowing cracked glass, and sat on a broken wooden seat watching as people tumbled in, jamming large wicker baskets filled with vegetables and exotic fruit into spaces that didn't exist. The young man next to me was carefully reading a newspaper upside down.

Letter

It's a tiny city, very easy to find your way about, shabby, gay and bustling, and although certainly not beautiful, it has great charm. I think if I flew straight in from Europe I wouldn't be impressed, but as I'm getting acclimatised, I like it. The population is only 800,000, which compared with the twelve million of Mexico City is nada.

Found my way to the Ticabus terminal, and bought a ticket from an amused, giggly man all the way to Panama. The bus goes to every capital in Central America, and you can get off in each place for as long as you like. The whole ticket cost £15, which is pretty good considering the distance, but I'm now short of money, even though I've been keeping within my budget of around £1–2 a day, everything included.

I was taken to an upmarket restaurant for a delicious dinner by the Dutch contact of a fellow traveller. Called Besthoff, he's THE man in Guatemala City as far as seaweed manufacturing is concerned, and didn't listen to a word I said. His wife is a nice, gawky German. We ate huge steaks, which was such a treat, as I've been living off bony fish for weeks. One of the volcanos outside the city was erupting, but sadly mist had come down so we couldn't see it.

It's odd hearing planes again. Been such a long time.

The cathedral has a wooden Christ hanging on the cross by only one arm. He looks more uncomfortable than usual, poor man, and there are bizarre Nativity figures, with plastic Santas strewn around the streets, still not helping me feel as if Christmas is just around the corner.

Tiny, abandoned Antigua – once the capital here, but destroyed by an earthquake in 1773, and still in ruins – is beautiful. Partly restored colonial houses, convents and churches fill the wonky cobbled streets where washerwomen were laying out sheets to dry. Overgrown gardens in cloisters give way to unbroken views of the volcanos and mountains around. I loved its laid-back atmosphere, but less the awful group of loud-mouthed American men who were knocking back pisco sours in the main square.

Back in Guatemala City, I'm sharing my room with Linda, an American air hostess who regales me with stories of her travels, and especially of the Cuna islands off Panama. I'd love to island hop. I want to see so much more than I can.

Longing to hear news from you, it's been over a month. If you get this in time, Happy Christmas and New Year…

I met several gringo travellers, veterans and dropouts from the war in Vietnam. They seemed lost and nervous in this land of firecrackers and backfiring vehicles, diving under tables or flinging themselves onto the floor whenever a noise surprised them, and in each other's company they drank heavily. Although ostensibly travelling around the country, they took absolutely no notice of where they were. Individually each man had his different stories, but collectively they shared exhausted, taut, vacant faces.

December 21st was the final day of a week-long fiesta for Santo Tomás in the hilltop village of Chichicastenango. Buses overflowed with a red sea of embroidery as locals piled in on top of me in the dusky light before dawn, to make the journey. They were all tiny compared to me, and solemn after the gaiety of Mexicans. We were stopped by police as we stuttered up and round steep, sharp bends high into the mountains, and ordered to get off the road; the president of Guatemala was coming up to the festival. After an hour waiting in the undergrowth with no sign of the presidential cavalcade, our driver yelled with anger and impatience, cranked up the engine, and we snorted off as fast as the old crock could trundle. I doubt that the president had any intention of coming.

Letter

How many times can one repeat how beautiful the countryside is, as every turn reveals another perfect view? Guatemala is like a precious jewel wrapped in soft paper, revealing its patina and brilliance as you unwrap the folds.

The tiny village of Chichicastenango boasts two white churches facing each other, one of which is Santo Tomás. Every weekend, locals flock up to Chichi for the market and for the church, where they chant in Mayan, burn candles and scatter flower petals. It's mysterious to watch, and especially so on this particular day, as Mayan religious beliefs blend with Catholicism. Folk saints are worshipped alongside Catholic ones. Cans of Coca-Cola and bottles of home-brewed alcohol are blessed. I can't imagine the dominance of Spanish Catholicism ever fully penetrating such intense paganism. Market stalls fill the entire village, laden with weavings and cloths, making it extremely difficult to pick your way through. Streets are packed solid with Mayans in all their finery, each one knee-high to a grasshopper. Tom Thumb would have felt like Gulliver. You would be fascinated, the day is unrelated to anything I've ever seen, the noise, colour, inebriation and freakiness of it all.

The narrow lanes of Chichi were already filled with drunks lying about the uneven muddy cobbles, in biting-cold, thin air which reeked of devoured or discarded stale alcohol. A watery sun was trying to see through the heavy grey clouds as exhausted women with children on their backs were either sleeping or propping up their husbands. Processions of masked dancers and discordant mariachi bands thronged the streets, while crude statues of Santo Tomás were carried high on wooden stretchers. He looked solemn as he was wobbled from side to side, undoubtedly praying that his sanctity would protect him from toppling into the disarray below. There was a dismal, sullen atmosphere as unhappy drunks staggered about when the music was melancholy, clutching each other for support, and then, when it perked up, they danced shambolically in an alcoholic haze.

I found a semblance of safety on the steps of the Santo Tomás church as two drunk little women pinioned themselves against my legs, and together we watched the processions swaying up and into the bowels of the ancient building. Priests wore short black smocks with intricately embroidered red headdresses as they too stumbled drunkenly up the steps. And then the rockets and firecrackers really got going, exploding everywhere. The din was deafening, there was no sense of where they were going to land, nor where the next ones would come bursting in from. Mostly made from bamboo filled with powder, they were launched at knee height, tearing into the crowds, damaging market stalls, but the throng was so tightly packed there was no escape. Like a Fellini nightmare it was both fascinating and frightening in equal measure. If any Viet vets had made the journey, they must have been deeply traumatised. I found it increasingly hard to stand still in the face of such an onslaught, so took refuge inside the church. My two Indian hangers-on slid, slumped to the ground when I moved, sleeping on through the uproar.

Inside was dark with vague shapes of people moving around, becoming faintly visible as my eyes acclimatised. Mayans were chanting as they lit candles, scattered flower petals and blessed bottles of alcohol which they emptied over the flowers. Priests wandered around in their extravagantly ornate garments, swigging mescal, the local lethal brew. Sombre music was played in the doorway by an out-of-tune, inebriated band, while back on the steps outside, tiny couples danced drunkenly in silence as night closed in.

After a long, hot three-hour wait for the Ticabus in a shabby, crowded terminal in Guatemala City, it finally turned up, spewed out its passengers and hooted impatiently for us to embark. Although air-conditioned and double-decker, it couldn't have been cleaned since its maiden voyage. The loos stank, rubbish covered the floors and my seat was so high that I could only glimpse an occasional flash of banana and coffee plantations out of the grimy window, as we roared east along the Pan-American Highway.

El Salvador

Happy Xmas (War Is Over)

Crossing the border into El Salvador took another three hours, my bag being the subject of much curiosity and speculation. My passport too was checked incessantly, almost as if no foreigners had ever passed through. To cap it all the bus broke down, then a tyre burst and it was dark by the time we limped into the city of San Salvador. I hadn't seen anything.

Brave as only the desperate can be, I found a call box and rang Federico. I had met him briefly for a drink in Mexico City, months earlier. He was male-model glamorous, had been on his way back to Salvador from a haircut with Vidal Sassoon in San Francisco. He spoke impeccable English with a broad Cockney accent.

First a maid answered, and I stuttered a message for him, sat on my bag and waited before trying again, convinced he had probably forgotten who I was. This time he answered, and immediately said he would come to the terminal and collect me.

'Come and stay for Christmas, it's the twenty-third of December.'

Grubby and tired, I waited under a rusty corrugated-iron roof on a side of the street thronged with bus passengers coming in, heading out, until a spotless Lancia sports car creamed up, and there he was: handsome, wavy dark hair, his clothes tailored to perfection.

'I kneew yew'd call me.'

He smiled as he opened the passenger door. He was sweating profusely, and emanated the most curious vibes; neither gay nor heterosexual. He had been educated in a melting pot of different countries and languages, spun around and gently landed here, in a small country in Central America. His apartment was predictably spacious and elegant. He had shower caps hanging on the back of his bathroom door, into which he folded his beautifully coiffed curls.

'I usually go to Neeew York for my haircut. Vidal is the ownly man I trust.'

I was puzzled by his Cockney accent. It felt so out of kilter with the rest of his carefully arranged appearance, and it wasn't until he told me his life story that I understood. His beloved governess was from the East End of London. It was she who had taught him English, and her strong accent had been embedded for thirty years, since he was three. And, of course, he had no idea that however grand his lifestyle, his accent perplexed several of those he hoped to impress. He was kind and funny, thoughtful, intelligent and far too beautiful.

Christmas Eve. The heat was intense, the sky luminous blue, as Franco, one of Federico's closest friends, purred up the gravel in his enormous 1950s car to collect us. He was half Ecuadorian and half Chilean, handsome with sparkling dark eyes and film-star teeth. We were off to the largest volcano in San Salvador, Izalco, to have lunch in a hotel built to watch over the firework displays of permanent eruptions, which gave the volcano its title: 'Beacon of the Sea'. As soon as the hotel construction was completed the eruptions ceased, and we stood on the rim gazing down into the depths of the dark crater, a paltry plume of smoke puffing out as if from a garden bonfire. Lava paths ran down the steep slopes under our feet as we looked out to the Pacific Ocean, hazy in the distance. From the other side we could see the hills of Honduras. A hubcap rolled off the wheel of our vintage car and raced us as we sped back down the dirt track, skidding round steep bends, heading for home.

That night felt as far away from any Christmas Eve I had ever known. No robins and snowmen, but cocktails in finest crystal, canapés off silver salvers, visiting different friends with Federico. There was attractive Pepe, whose wife had shot herself a few months earlier. His house was like a museum, filled with treasures, especially owls: marble, bronze, stuffed. He believed they brought wisdom and good luck. The latter had evaded him, but he played the guitar and sang. Tortured and sad, he poured out his heart when we sat together. I wanted to hold him in my arms and thought about him for a long while afterwards.

Off we whirled, Federico propelling me along with his hand under my elbow, to visit more friends, beautiful international women, friendly in the knowledge that they were clever, cultured and would never dream of travelling the way I did. I talked to a sprightly old man who had lived in Paris in the twenties and known Picasso, Sartre, Isadora Duncan and Cocteau. 'When are you coming back?' he asked. 'Please come back.'

As midnight approached, people peeled off to go to Mass, children were dragged along in party clothes, ancient aunts, grandparents, all ages were up and celebrating. Federico was dancing spectacularly, alone, shaking his hips, shimmying to 'La Bamba'. I wanted to go on watching him, but he stopped and insisted we listen to the songs from *My Fair Lady* before he took me to yet another friend. I suppose 'The Rain in Spain' was appropriate. We arrived at a monstrously hideous house, floodlit by its glaring swimming pool illuminations, filled with a stunning art collection. Along with the friend sat an old aunt, dolled up like a pantomime dame. They were expecting at least fifty people to turn up, but as nobody came, I got uncontrollable giggles while the four of us sat forlornly outside, sweltering as we struggled to make polite conversation, until Auntie was taken home, and we escaped the oppressive emptiness.

Four o'clock on Christmas morning, overwhelmed by the kindness of so many strangers, I collapsed, exhausted, into bed.

Letter to my parents on Christmas Day

The parties started again at lunchtime, lounging round the swimming pool, eating turtle doves' eggs and caviar, followed by cold stuffed turkey with salads, at little tables under bougainvillea.

I kept thinking of you in England, wondering where you were, and what you were doing. No wrapping up warm and going for a muddy walk here. It's more about dressing up as best I can, or stripping off into my only, shabby bikini, struggling to convince myself I can look almost stylish. I'll never ever forget Christmas lunch 1974. The opulence felt unreal after spending so many days and nights on antiquated buses, and yet everyone I met was warm and generous, sweeping me up in a sort of Salvadorian dream.

Elizabeth, beautiful wife of Luis, wore a large jade and gold necklace, plus bracelet, which she'd had set in Paris. She flirted outrageously with every man, passing a small gold star from her tongue to theirs. I almost had to take it from Federico and backed off just in time. He passed it on to Pepe, and I was confused.

'Geewd mornin,' whispered Federico at 4am, just giving me time to throw on some clothes, and to say goodbye to my extravagant days in his little country, to hug such a generous, immaculate friend, before taking a taxi back to reality.

On the way to the Ticabus terminal, we passed a man lying dead in the road, his body twisted, his face squashed down, a pool of blood underneath.

Reflecting on the past few days, saying adios to such a magnanimous, thoughtful man affected me. I hadn't realised how much it meant to be looked after and nurtured unconditionally. I must have looked a wreck in my faded clothes and yet, knowing nothing about my life, Federico had introduced me to his sophisticated friends, and included me in all he did, without hesitation. The country was ricocheting politically, with attempted coups and rigged elections. Inequality was leading to increased unrest, and attempts at redistributing large landholdings amongst the peasant population had failed. (According to statistics, 77% of arable land belonged to 0.01% of the population.) There were protests and massacres, but much worse was to come; between 1979 and 1992, civil war raged in El Salvador, with thousands killed and disappeared. And as everywhere, only the rich got out in time.

I slept, we stopped somewhere for breakfast and, still exhausted, I struggled to prise my eyes open and catch the green countryside as it flashed by. The sight of the dead man played like a broken record in my head, while an irritating American couple sat in front of me. She overflowed her seat and talked trivia loudly, incessantly.

Honduras

Coming Around Again

We hung around in heavyweight humidity at the border with Honduras, where I paid $1 to enter the country, and after scouring my bible, the brand-new *1974 South American Handbook*, which contained every country in Latin America, I decided to roll on through. It told me that Honduras was the most backward of all Central American republics. 70% of the population didn't wear shoes, more than 55% were illiterate, 60% of children were born to unmarried mothers. Education was compulsory but most of the rural children had no school to go to. There were few paved roads. None of that had put me off, but the north had torrid jungle swamps, abandoned ports, excellent Panama hats. Dysentery and stomach parasites were prevalent.

Appealing wasn't a word that sprang to mind, and the capital, Tegucigalpa, was notoriously unsafe. For a brief moment I perked up, reading that the painter Velásquez had been born here. But reading the small print, he turned out not to be the famous Spaniard Diego (Velázquez), but José, a very different talent.

Letter

We crossed the Continental Divide, where water splits, and rivers flow on one side into the Atlantic, the other into the Pacific, but all around us the countryside looked hot as hell, desolate and windy. Honduras is desperately poor, malaria is rife, and in September this year a cyclone killed over eight thousand people. The only railway lines are privately owned by huge banana plantations.

Nicaragua

We Gotta Get Out Of This Place

The humidity was unrelenting as we reached the Nicaraguan border. I stuck to my seat, to my clothes, and dripped as we all hung around outside for interminable hours at the checkpoint, while power-hungry customs men fingered the contents of our bags and rifled through documents on the ubiquitous broken wooden tables. Finally allowed through, we rattled past cotton, coffee and fruit plantations, green fields with floppy-eared cows which bizarrely, apart from the palm trees, reminded me of England. We passed grey snake-like Lake Managua, eerie and uninviting, home to freshwater bull sharks, swordfish and alligators, surrounded by equally unfriendly shale and spiky rock.

On along the Pan-American Highway, a misleading name for a narrow potholed lane with barely enough space for two cars to pass, much of it unpaved. Without warning, Managua bus station rose up to throttle us, living up to all expectations of squalor.

Letter

Since the earthquake of 1972, much of the city has been destroyed, so that it's all in bits, and spread out like smashed crockery. I could only find a real dump to sleep in for the night, with a stable door and no roof. It was exorbitant, no loo anywhere on the premises, not even a hole in the ground, and the awful American's voice droned on from some dark corner. It was eight at night, the downtown area is badly lit and dangerous, but I found a call box which worked, and rang Lucia, whom I'd met over Christmas in San Salvador, who adorably came straight round and took me out of the hellhole for supper. She's beautiful, about twenty-four, lives here with her father, has to be chaperoned if she goes out (she had to bring a maid with her), isn't allowed to drive or travel by herself, and was so envious of me being able to travel without my parents. She was fascinated by my stories of life in London, amazed that women can work! And of course her life in captivity really reminded me to appreciate my astonishing freedom, and the luck of being born into a family which lets me spread my wings and fly. Sadly, although she wanted to show me her country, I had already booked the bus for early the following morning. Couldn't face another night in the dump. She was horrified that I'd landed there, and unnecessarily apologetic for the general chaos. Hardly her fault.

As it turned out, this was a lucky decision. The next day, guerrillas indiscriminately opened fire all around the crowded bus station, killing scores of people. They apparently murdered a minister, and are holding twelve people hostage. I met some Brazilians later who said they'd had a tough time getting out: there was an immediate curfew and the border was closed for several days. The Cubans apparently claimed responsibility.

Nicaragua had been ruled, with ruthless, corrupt control, by the Somoza family for just over thirty-eight years. Widespread poverty, repression and inequality remained constant. Five years after I was there, in 1979, there was a revolution, in which the Sandinistas, led by Daniel Ortega, established a revolutionary government, and an estimated fifty thousand people lost their lives.

Costa Rica

Forever Young

Another relentlessly long drive heading for Costa Rica. More hours in dense humidity hanging around at the border. I was shattered, once more barely able to prise my eyes open and watch, as we juddered past coffee and the eternal banana plantations. San José couldn't come a moment too soon.

I was beyond thankful to leave the bus, with the bossy, over-made-up woman next to me yapping like a Pekinese at her equally irritating son. He stuck his tongue out at me whenever she wasn't looking. I could have slapped them both, and splashed out $4 for a night in a room with its own shower that even had hot water. Having scrubbed off the grime of several days, and pummelled clothes into a messy pulp, I wandered along neat streets, amazed at smart shops, new cars and a startlingly pale population. It felt odd there were no Indigenous people visible. 'All killed by the Spanish conquistadors,' muttered a man. 'Intermarried,' hissed another. Neither was there any of the terrible humidity which had dogged my previous days.

Letter

San José is a breath of fresh air. Small, neat, clean with lots of good shops and restaurants, although Americanised with cardboard hamburgers and tasteless milkshakes. I'm suddenly on another planet, tired from non-stop changes in altitudes and humidity, not to mention hard seats, and bloated from a diet of biscuits and stodge. I've covered 1,052 miles from the Mexico–Guatemala border. It will be 1,604 in Panama.

Went to the British Embassy to collect my mail, but it was closed, so deep disappointment, and my book, *The Teachings of Don Juan*, doesn't grip me. He has dreams he can fly, which I've often had too.

I haven't yet seen an attractive Costa Rican, and the guidebook says they're the most beautiful people in the world. I tried the National Theatre. Pretty but shut. So went to the cinema, and watched the latest Bond movie, *Live and Let Die*, packed with teenyboppers screaming with fright. So very British, it makes being here even weirder. I returned to the embassy the following day. Still shut. Misery.

Boarding one of five small wooden carriages of the great Northern Railway steam train, I sat on a bench surrounded by Afro-Caribbeans and felt happier again. They were heading home for new year, and laughed as they chatted to each other in pidgin English, which was fun to listen to although I couldn't understand more than one word in ten. Just enough to keep me hooked. Agwe explained in Spanish that they had come over from Jamaica decades ago to work on the railway, and on banana and coffee plantations. Many had stayed on, marrying and settling in the north with their families. Friendly, and curious as to where I had come from, they appeared huge as they sang together in mellifluous deep voices. After being amongst tiny Indigenous people for the past months, I was fascinated by their size.

We were leaving San José and chugging north, through neat plantations, interspersed with rolling fields of well-fed cattle. The train kept pace alongside a gushing river, often high above it, before descending so close that I could almost reach out and cool my hands. We passed small towns of wooden houses on stilts, children playing, their ample mothers gossiping beside washing draped over verandahs. Tethered horses fidgeted nearby. The countryside was beguiling, lush and green, turning to tangled jungle as we neared the coast. I saw a three-toed sloth hanging from vine-covered branches on a tree, watching lugubriously as flocks of brightly coloured birds fluttered in all directions. The men next to me were teasing a friend who had so many bottles of gin he couldn't hold them all, and at each jolt, one would roll off under the benches, which caused much merriment and more laughter as he crawled around trying to retrieve it.

Six hours later I felt like Butch Cassidy as I picked my way over the narrow-gauge tracks, and out into the only street of Puerto Limón, a potholed, muddy lane. I'd hoped to take a photograph of the steam engine for my train-obsessed younger brother, but it had disconnected itself from the carriages and puffed away before I'd even got out.

The Pensión Costa Rica was run by two toothless wonders, possibly sisters, but we couldn't find a mutual word of communication. They gabbled at me, waving knotted fingers attached to scrawny arms as they shuffled round an old house on the verge of falling down, replete with cockroaches, mosquitoes and bats. My room had a stable door with no window, where I spent most of the time chasing beetles round the filthy floor trying to crunch them under my flimsy flip-flops, flapping madly and ineffectually at the clouds of insects. A view of the Caribbean Sea from the rubbish-strewn, broken-down garden revealed dismally grey water, and the small port was disappointing and dirty. It felt stuck in a time warp, unchanged since the end of the banana boom of the 1800s, although two cargo boats tied up alongside the cracked pier gave me a twinge of nostalgia. They symbolised an adventure into the unknown, a memory of a *bonne bouche* before the main event, whereas now I was involved with the menu.

The small Chinese community who remained had also been brought in to work on the railway. Their names adorned little restaurants by the sea offering chow mein and other exotic dishes. But I had cashed my last traveller's cheque, and this paltry amount would have to last me until I reached Ecuador. So I bought avocados and bananas from women with bottoms as broad as continental shelves, from emaciated women wearing woolly hats in the heat, and from muscly men in ripped vests. We laughed together under the now-pouring rain, and wished each other a happy new year.

Back in my airless, sticky, creepy-crawly room, a humid deluge outside, rotting stable door flapping, I hunted for rusty nails stuck into damp concrete walls on which to hang my wet clothes, wondering where family and friends were on the cusp of this coming new year. Not for the first time I felt far away from everyone I knew, and was asleep by 8.30pm.

1st January 1975

The train returning to San José took hours longer, as it chugged slowly uphill. A man sitting opposite stared unblinking and wide-eyed at me for most of the journey, while he frantically rubbed his knees, and eventually limped across to talk to me. By this time I was embarrassed, uncertain where to look, wishing I had someone else with me. But he was a gentle man, spoke good Spanish, and wanted no more than to assure me that Costa Rican police keep screwdrivers in their holsters so they can unscrew number plates of cars with parking offences.

I was famished when we finally arrived and headed straight to McDonald's for a Big Mac, chips, apple pie and Coke. I could hardly believe what I was doing, but at this time there was only one McDonald's in England, with ashtrays on the Formica tables, and despite the publicity I had never been. In a café I wrote letters home on fine blue airmail paper, clearing my conscience with postcards to friends, and catching up on my journal. I'd hardly started when the waitress came up and said a man on another table was paying for my drink. I left. It had been a long day.

'Do you need a weeza?' asked the blonde German in a queue for the Ticabus tickets, but my thoughts were on getting to the bloody British Embassy to retrieve my mail, and I fled. Finally, it was open, and at last I had letters, contact with my other world. In England many friends were struggling, and berating the tough state of the country. A three-day working week was in operation, the past year had inflicted two general elections, IRA bombings on the mainland,

and businesses collapsing. I read an unsettling, bitter letter from my mother about my father, and how unhappy she was. And luckily, amongst others, an uplifting one from my grandfather, who had shown my letters thus far to the commissioning editor of John Murray Publishers, who expressed strong interest in my writing a book on these travels when I returned. I reread them all many times. They were the closest I could get to hearing familiar voices.

Returning to the Pensión Illimani, the husky old owner informed me I'd had a message from an American who was coming to take me out to lunch. Mr Swett had received my card – he, an unknown friend of a friend, arrived late, having thought the dive was called Easy Money, and wondering who he was about to pick up. I scrambled into his truck and was whirled up into the hills above San José to his finca, with views over the mountains, and his hilarious wife in flowing kaftan. 'Can you imagine having a name like Swett?' she laughed. 'I've refused to say sweat all my life – it's called perspiration. And then I go and marry him. It's so embarrassing.' They appeared to have houses scattered around the world, and Swett seemed to me a small word to have to say. I was fed like a goose being prepped for foie gras, and as afternoon turned to dusk, they loaded me with food, and took me to catch the night Ticabus for Panama. They were the epitome of a happy couple, full of stories about their coconut chips business here, their house in Antigua, their ranch in America. Such friendly generosity and sense of fun was contagious, and I settled happily back in an extra-hard seat for the final leg of my bus journey through Central America, rumbling sixteen hours through the night, grateful for my fortunate encounters, excited and content, although Chile, and my university friends, were still a long way off.

Panama

Tous Les Garçons Et Les Filles

We reached the border as the sun rose into a hazy sky, momentarily turning clouds into pink candyfloss. Then reality kicked in and knocked out all sentimental metaphors. Ordered off the bus, we had to hang around in oppressive humidity for several hours before there was any sign of life from border police.

Letter

Ordered again to queue, we shuffled through a terrifying passport check, with passengers being waved away, growled at, and some refused entry. In order to enter Panama everyone must have a ticket out, which I had in the form of a flight ticket to Quito, and a minimum of $200 on them. By this time I was out of traveller's cheques, and had $9 on me in the whole world. Typically, the man doing the checks was a nightmare, insisting each person prove everything, going through their bags with a toothcomb. The girl in front of me was asked to show her ticket and traveller's cheques, and then it was my turn. He rifled through my case, then demanded my documents. Shaking like a leaf I showed my ticket, and said I had $300 on me. He stared at me, and by some miracle didn't ask me to show him the money. He wrote the amount in my passport and waved me through. Relief, until he called me back, by which time I was really scared, but it turned out he'd put the wrong date in my passport and had to re-stamp it. Such a narrow escape, and God knows what would have happened if he'd caught me.

Back on the bus, on repeat with heat and humidity, views of the sea, stilt houses, and gauchos on horses, whirling lassos, rounding up cattle. Then American signs started to appear, and as we trundled over the impressive Bridge of the Americas, which spans the entrance to the Panama Canal, vast American and Panamanian flags flew proudly in the breeze, as a spectacular panorama of the river, filled with ships, spread out in front of us.

Downtown, the tiny Hotel Ideal was far from living up to its name. But I'd tramped the streets for miles in sticky, sweaty heat looking for something I could afford, when I came across an old man from Birmingham sweltering on the pavement in a shabby patched suit, living in Panama for thirty years, who led me to this dive. My tiny room with an apology of a balcony, overlooked the heavily guarded president's palace, where I spotted droopy white flamingos creeping around marble pillars in the presidential gardens.

A friend in London had given me the number of an English couple he vaguely knew living in Panama, and once settled I called them out of curiosity, hoping perhaps to meet for a drink. I had no idea who they were, and they'd certainly never heard of me. 'Come and stay,' said Fiona immediately.

Letter

Panama itself is a pretty country, hilly with stubbly fields becoming jungly near the coast. I'd been dreading Panama City as had heard so many horror stories about it from fellow travellers, but curiously I like it. There's a wonderful old part, Panamá Viejo, which must be like New Orleans in the 1920s. Wooden houses with balconies; intimate; seedy; *Streetcar-Named-Desire*-full of bustle and character.

Then there are the remnants of Fort San Lorenzo, mainly in ruins, which was frequently attacked by Drake and then by Henry Morgan, the infamous '*piratas ingleses*' who plundered Spanish galleons laden with treasure. New Panama, where I'm staying, is where the shops, offices, residential areas are. Everywhere you can see the sea, and ships waiting. It really does feel like the crossroads of the world.

The canal too is fascinating. As you know, the Americans own it, including three miles either side the entire length of the country, which really splits Panama in two. There's a series of locks at each end, an unbelievable engineering feat, and intriguing to see queues of vast liners and heavily laden cargo ships being towed in, rising up and down with the changing water levels before gliding on out to sea. The canal between each lock is a series of natural lakes, linked together, jungle right down to the water, which the Americans keep constantly dredged. It's extraordinary seeing so many ships steaming through them.

Another letter

Yesterday I took the American-run train which has a loud Western hoot-whistle, American guards, and runs beside the canal all the way from the Pacific to Colón, the northern port and Atlantic entrance to the canal. The journey was fascinating, but Colón is pretty dirty and scruffy, a larger version of Puerto Limón and a free-zone, so filled with tacky duty-free shops. When I got back to Panama, I thought I'd save my remaining few dollars and find a bus, so started walking down a main street when a man came up to me and asked if I wanted any help, where was I going… I stuck my nose in the air and walked on, whereupon he flashed a police card at me and explained he was a detective, that this particular street was renowned for thieves and mugging, and although it was broad daylight, I should take a taxi. He waited until I'd scrambled into one. So nice of him to have bothered. I would never have known, until too late.

Another letter

It's bliss to be in a comfortable flat, and so generously looked after. I had a real bath for the first time since Mexico while Maria and Chica, the two maids, washed and ironed everything I possess. Christopher and Fiona are full of fun, and it's a marvellous break from the pokey little one-night holes – particularly as it's desperately hot, and so humid even the cars need air conditioning. I get a free sauna every time I walk outside. Christopher is big, blonde and laughs a lot. He does something with insurance which doesn't seem to occupy much of his time, and Fiona is incredibly English. They've got sweet little Miss Moppet, their two-year-old daughter, who reaches up to hold my hand. I guess I haven't ever come into close contact with children, so we are rather intrigued with each other.

They drove me around old Panama at night, around the cobbled streets and beautiful floodlit cathedral. We had dinner outside by the sea at Club Panama and ate revolting celery stuffed with tinned cheese muck, followed by delicious fish with almonds.

I schlepped off to the British Embassy, but no letters for me. Hopefully there'll be news in Quito. Great excitement, I fly early tomorrow morning. South America at last, and that's where the travelling really begins. The distances will be huge; Central America seems big enough. I'm sad to be missing Colombia, but I've come across travellers going the other way, and two were heavily bandaged, as they'd had their wrists slashed to steal their cameras and watches. The country sounds lawless, and just too dangerous at the moment to contemplate travelling, although in reality I'm rarely alone, there is almost always another traveller heading in the same direction.

There was still time to board a ferry to tiny Taboga Island for the day, heading out under the Bridge of the Americas, past sharks and ships waiting to go through the canal, past an island with isolated leprosy colony still in use. There were no cars on Taboga, only a footpath leading to a neat village filled with sweet-smelling flowers around which miniscule turquoise and green hummingbirds hovered. Inside the beautifully decorated Iglesia de San Pedro, second-oldest church in the western hemisphere, I read about the bones of pirates interred within its walls, and I learned that the artist Paul Gauguin spent several weeks on the island, recovering from malaria.

By five the following morning, kind Christopher was driving me to Panama airport, where I was to fly with Braniff International to Ecuador. The plane was on its way from Miami to Quito, before going on to Lima and Santiago. The crew wore Pucci.

SOUTH AMERICA AT LAST: ECUADOR AND THE GALÁPAGOS ISLANDS

Morning Has Broken

Appalled at having to pay an exit tax of $4 to leave Panama, I raised my spirits hoovering through every crumb of an enormous breakfast on the plane, pressing my face to the window as we neared Quito, clouds parting enough to see we were surrounded by velvety mountains so close our wings must surely have been touching them. We meandered through fertile volcanos and hills, eventually touching down at 9,500 feet. South America at last.

I had failed to get a visa, and was apprehensive about the notoriously beady-eyed customs and immigration officers. But they looked more officious than they were, waving me on through and out into the cobbled streets of Quito.

El Dorado, the cheapest *pensión* in the city, was perfectly situated between the old and the new. It seemed too good to be true until later, when I realised it was filled with lecherous drunk men and rented out by the hour. But I was in a hurry to reach the Bank of London and South America, or BOLSA as it was known, to collect a new batch of traveller's cheques, and it was only by the time I returned, dusk descended, that I fully grasped the purpose of my lodgings. Firmly locking the door I pored over maps, studied the *South American Handbook*, and spent a sleepless night hearing nothing but creaks, shrieks and groans through paper-thin walls.

Quito's streets were filled with Indigenous people trotting, not walking, around in the high-altitude thin air. Men with ruddy skin, bent under the weight of their bulky loads, sported thick black plaits hanging down their backs. They had appealing faces with prominent cheekbones, impenetrable dark eyes, and although small, they were not as wrinkled as the Mayans I had seen. I was excited to be in South America, but already missing the bright colours of previous countries. Ecuador was embracing me with a sombre, brooding blanket.

The bus journey to Otavalo, two hours away, gave me my first real glimpse of Ecuadorian countryside, gentle in colouring, majestic in scale. Subtle blues, sage greens, burnt umbers blended with adobe huts moulding into the landscape. A vast azure sky full of puffy clouds surrounded colossal mountains; extinct volcanos covered in dark green moss-like grass soared above trees and cultivation on the lower slopes.

The Otavalenos were purported to be the cleanest Indigenous people in Ecuador. Men wore trilby hats, blue ponchos and bare feet. Women had big bosoms, narrow shoulders and displayed thick rows of colourful homemade beads. A wonderful sight, as they too jogged rather than walked around.

Down by the lake women were washing their clothes and hair in the juice of the penca cactus, which transformed well-worn homespun cotton into dazzling white, while all around young children paddled in the soapy water carrying baby siblings on their slender backs.

Searching, unsuccessfully, for a much-talked-about cockfight, I met a foreign couple walking in the square who offered me a lift back to Quito. They turned out to be Hungarian refugees who had settled in Ecuador. Olga had a sad, hard face. Disillusioned with life, she spoke entirely in Spanish. Carlos was gentle, smiley, and back at their home in the city he lent me books on Aztecs, Mayans, Incas. They were a lonely pair.

Returning late to the Dorado dump I was told by a heavily made-up woman in the hall that an *amigo rubio* (blonde) was staying here and looking for me. Horror of horrors. This was a man who had threatened to join me somewhere along my route, and was confident he would easily find me. I didn't know him well, and decent as he was, I remembered him as the caricature of a jolly good Englishman. Splendid.

The following morning I crept out of the hotel alongside girls with smudged black around lifeless eyes, carrying tatty cloth bags out of which poked tools of their trade, convinced I was bound to bump into Gordon. But the coast was clear, and I made it along narrow streets to a crossing, where Carlos the Hungarian was waiting in his car to take me into the countryside.

Letter

Three hours through unimaginable scenery – towering mountains, stampeding rivers overflowing into waterfalls, tiny Indigenous villages, snow-covered volcanos and lush tropical vegetation. Sliding along a road that was boulder strewn and more than half washed away by landslides, a haphazard shanty town suddenly appeared, like an apparition out of the mist. In the middle of this nowhere, we had lunch: a gristly, limp soup – better not to know what was in it, but my long-suffering stomach stood up to it, and we set off again down cramped tracks, car wipers useless against the onslaught of torrential rain, until we were way off the so-called main road. Eventually we came to a little clearing, abandoned the car and squelched off on foot for a couple of miles down narrow paths hemmed in by thick jungle, occasionally interrupted with small banana plantations. We had to cross ferocious rivers (it's the rainy season, so all rivers are now in flood) by crude bridges, mostly a couple of slippery logs lashed together. As you know my head for heights isn't great, and wobbling over in the pelting rain was quite a feat of facing my fears. We came across numerous groups of horses with wooden saddles standing sodden amidst profusions of wildflowers and long, wet grasses.

And eventually we made it to our destination, Santo Domingo, the main village of an almost extinct tribe called the Colorados, who are naked from the waist up and paint their bodies in stripes. Men put mud and achiote seeds (with which they make a red dye) on their hair, which is then rendered cardboard-stiff. The backs of their heads are shaved upwards, and sometimes topped with a little hat like a flowerpot. They also use achiote, which comes from a local palm, to ward off evil. We met the chief who flashed gold teeth at us, slightly spoiling the illusion of finding an almost untouched tribe. They were all sheltering from the rain under enormous gunnera-like leaves which they held high as perfect umbrellas, some wearing wellington boots which looked incongruous with their stripy bodies, and insisted that we sat under the dripping overhang of a thatch roof, where we watched pigs rootle around datura bushes laden with yellow and pink bell-like flowers. They use the root of this as a drug. Huts are the usual adobe, a mixture of clay, sand, water and straw, moulded into bricks and dried in the sun. Here they are built around a compound where there is an albino witch doctor who has earned so much money he has to have four bodyguards. But gradually people are drifting to the towns, and only a thousand or so are left in the jungle.

We smiled and stared at each other, but having no language we could share, Carlos and I slithered all the way back to the car, clambering once more over huge slippery fallen tree trunks to cross rivers – I've never been wetter in my life. The drive back to Quito was hairy as the mist had come down, the car steamed up, and Carlos overtook on blind corners, of which there were plenty, directing his aim at the deepest potholes.

Gordon was waiting. I never discovered how he'd tracked me down, but here he was, blonde and so bloody English. A man in the mix and goodbye to help from kind strangers, or offers of a seat on a crowded train.

Days filled with visits. To the Equator line where an ugly concrete pillar marked the centre of the world, bullied by barren mountains looming large behind. To impoverished villages where brightly coloured figures made of bread were painstakingly put together by hands gnarled with age and manual labour. In Quito there were numerous churches and museums alongside colonial houses in need of paint, dominating the streets, while terrible smells of pee and cooking fat permeated the thin air. Local markets seemed occupied only by the maimed and injured Indians. Worst of all, when I reached the *pensión* at the end of one long day, I discovered someone had been in my room, had been sick down the side of the bed, and all over the so-called bathroom down the passage. In the next-door room Peg Leg Ronaldo was having a drunken party which lasted through the night, until the hooting, honking, belching traffic started up again in the early hours of a new day.

I was up and out of grotty El Dorado by 4.30 on a cold pitch-black morning, wearing every item of warm clothing I possessed.

The station was almost deserted as Gordon and I hung around waiting. The only train to the coast left Quito three times a week; a converted bus had been put on tracks and comfortably transported passengers on its narrow gauge for the twelve-hour journey to Guayaquil. A few gringos stumbled onto the platform as the bus-train arrived and we each dragged our dusty, battered bags on board.

The sun rose as we left Quito behind, and threw golden light over fertile valleys with patchwork-quilt fields. Cotopaxi loomed over us, a still-active volcano sparkling under its mantle of white snow in the sunshine. Out of the window, treeless and spectacular hills looked red-grey, soft green-blue, a giant wild world. Men with guns walked, or rode horses, their dogs barking at the train while it endlessly hooted as we crossed lanes and highways. Twice we had to stop in a siding to let a steam engine rattle past, magnificently black and shiny, with gleaming brass, as it hauled its heavy load. An old British engine still used by the banana plantations.

Startled brightly coloured birds rushed off, muddy rivers were in flood, adobe huts huddled together. Then came the Devil's Nose, where we sped along the edge of a precipice so high that the station way down below looked as if it must be on another planet. We stopped, shunted and reversed backwards down hairpin bends, crossed rickety bridges. An exhilarating roller coaster.

Letter

For six of the twelve hours I sat on the roof of the train. I wanted a wider view of the incredible landscape, so climbed up and joined the luggage, held tight and swallowed my nerves. The worst of the hair-raising moments was when another tunnel suddenly appeared without warning, and I had to lie totally flat, with only a few inches above my face to spare. Otherwise it was thrilling, passing monumental mountains rearing up to over twelve thousand feet, hanging on as best I could as we hurtled round bends and gazed down at foaming rivers in spate miles below. It's the first time I've ridden on top of a train. If I'd thought about it, I'm not sure I would have done it, as the journey was full of so many potential disasters. But there was no one to stop me.

As we neared the coast, land flattened out into paddy fields and more banana plantations. Humidity kicked in, and as the little train slowed, the sky was filled with flashing shards of colour as more tropical birds swirled around us. I finally scrambled down off the roof, into the energy-sapping heavy weight of oppressively hot air.

We had at last arrived in Guayaquil, which is larger than Quito, the industrial business centre, and it's gruesome. Filled with black smoke from all the steam trains, it appears sticky and dirty, lacking charm of any sort, except for its huge famous cemetery which is poignant and unexpectedly beautiful. The city sits fifty miles up a gloopy river from the sea.

I had contact details of the consul there, but hadn't been in touch, so when Kingsley's chauffeur met us off the train, having been brushed aside by Gordon who thought he was an annoying taxi driver, there was an awkward altercation. He had a card in his hand saying that I should go with him. But I couldn't just leave Gordon, so he came too. It turned out Kingsley and Moll had been tipped off by a business friend in England, and had invited me to stay with them for three days until I set off for the Galápagos Islands, but I had only a vague idea of this plan, and had an uncomfortably frosty reception turning up with an uninvited man. I was squirming with embarrassment until they reluctantly agreed he could also stay. (To which Gordon replied, 'Golly, that's kind. Splendid.')

Letter

Kingsley is the Brit consul, BOLSA rep and everything else he can lay his hands on. They are very rafeened, she talks about the servants, taking *The Taymes*. It's hard work, as apart from having to leap out of the way of the clock's cuckoo which springs shrieking from its house into the middle of the room, I feel obliged to admire their furniture, their family photos, be extra polite all the time. It's sticky in every way. But they are so good to have us to stay, and to feed us so well. She leaves apple paay, swiftly covered with ants, when they go out to duplicate bridge, almost every night.

Journal

Having finished his jigsaw puzzle, Kingsley gave us a gayded tour of his office (thrills), and after collecting Molly from her tennis club, quite a sight in white shorts and jockey cap, we went off to lunch and swim at the country club, where K plays golf. He spent the entire time telling me about birdies and tweeters and getting things under par. I hadn't a clue what he was on about. That evening they took us to the Union Club where we clinked glasses and cheerios, discussed common peeps, glayciers, sugar refaynaries through the tropical night. It transpires Moll and Kingsley have spent fifteen years in a mining town in Peru, six years in Belize and five here. They are pure expat snobs, and wouldn't dream of having us to stay if I didn't know his boss in England although, either way, it's incredibly kind of them.

Letter

We left them for a few days and went off by bus to a godforsaken place called Playas. Basically a beach with mangrove swamps, leafless trees and a few little houses dotted around. I'd eaten something that didn't agree with me and felt sick most of the time. Couldn't swim because of the sharks, and the beach was mud rather than sand. After a long walk around the bay evading the filth, human excrement, scabby, wretched dogs, I settled on a rough wooden bench in the shade of a palm-roofed beach shack where, after an interminable wait, disgusting watery soup, soggy rice and fish bones arrived. I left it all and felt worse.

The sun sank low above the Pacific, clouds blazed vivid pinks as I watched fishing boats laden almost level with the sea, followed by a billowing swarm of frigatebirds. Fish and shrimps were transferred from bigger boats to one-man balsa-wood rafts and dugouts, a few logs lashed together. Paddled by hand they had one large sail, and being so light, skimmed fast along the frothy white caps of the rolling waves, their pale ochre colour now catching and glinting crimson and pink in the setting sun. Men stripped to the waist, women with skirts pulled up around their knees crowded round as the boats glided up onto the beach. And out to sea silhouettes of birds filled the sky, diving for food. Pelicans swallowed large fish in one enormous gulp.

Journal

Talking of gulping, Gordon drives me nearly mad with his. It seems everything he puts in his mouth is slurped, sucked or gobbled. I wish I had earplugs and am annoyed I mind so much.

Back in Guayaquil, I bought Sir eau de cologne for Kingsley, and dusting powder for Moll, before they drove us down to the new port to find *Iguana*, our home for the next couple of weeks. She was an old Canadian corvette, recently redesigned as a small cruiser to take passengers around the Galápagos Islands. Moll came because she wanted to have a good snoop around, and sniffed dismissively as she peered into my narrow dark cabin. 'Bit like a miniature couchette on the trayn with British Rayl,' she snapped. Gordon was to sleep on a mattress squished on the narrow strip of floor, as of course he hadn't booked to come on the trip and there was nowhere else. We said our goodbyes, each safe in the knowledge that none of us would ever meet again. Cuckoo.

Letter

The boat was compact, and the fifty passengers and thirty-five crew melted away. She had several small decks with long chairs and sets of binoculars, always somewhere to get away from people. We sailed that evening and had two full days at sea, good for getting sea legs back and to meet our fellow passengers. There were twenty Canadians from a zoological society, a few German biology students, some hilarious old biddies, a fabulous family of ten from Brazil, and the only other Brit, a zoo director.

Infuriatingly for me, and much to everyone else's entertainment, the captain had a crush on me and would never leave me alone. As soon as I sat down anywhere I'd hear 'Sarita', and he'd beetle along to sit next to me.

Typically Latin, he was small and frightfully dapper. He had the self-satisfied smug smile of a man with a mistress in the port, a wife at home, and anyone he could find along the way would be most welcome. Gordon was thrilled as Capitano was constantly buying me drinks, asking me to sit at his table where there was free wine, so he, Gordon, like a faithful Labrador, tagged along, happy to make the most of this profitable liaison. Hiding from my pursuer became a game of hide-and-seek, aided by the rest of the amused passengers, and a great icebreaker. We were soon firm friends with academics from Toronto and old trouts from Missouri. I had nicknames for everyone. He, the creep, was the Vermilion Flycatcher.

There was Hot Spot, the handsome young Belgian first mate. Good-looking from a distance, and an infinitely better proposition, not that I had any choice in the matter. He welcomed me into the tiny, old-fashioned bridge gleaming with polished brass, and talked to us all in the cool of the evening about the history of the Galápagos Islands: how they were formed by gas and air pushing up from under the seabed, discovered by the Bishop of Panama in the 1500s, used by pirates who introduced destructive goats and rats, then took turtles away for fresh meat, as they could survive eighteen months without food. British whalers created a post office, and eventually Charles Darwin founded his theory of evolution, based on what he discovered on the islands: the adaptation of animal life to its surroundings.

The following day at sea was rough and overcast. Weighed down by a blanket of humidity, I watched whales spouting, incredulous at the size of their monumental backs as they rose sedately, breaching the surface, then gracefully back down under. There were shoals of flying fish and hundreds of small storm petrels flying low over the angry water.

Back inside I played chess with my pursuer, who plied me with strong Martinis, insisting I sit with him at lunch while he filled my glass with wine. Lech, lech, I could read his simple plan, but managed to extricate myself and fled into the bowels of the churning boat to my bunk, where I sweltered in the stuffy heat, unable to open the porthole swamped by waves. I felt sick.

Dolphins leapt out of the mist in pairs to welcome the new dawn and our arrival off the island of San Cristóbal. Leaning over the side we could see fish of all shapes and sizes, stripy, mottled, bright greens and yellows, electric blues, huge eels. It was as clear as watching fish in a tank. A frisson of excitement echoed round the boat as old Sparrow talked nonsense, Liberace appeared in a new suit, The Heron shouted loudly and Hot Spot fell overboard. Everyone gathered cameras, hats, and disembarked in small prearranged groups to potter along the only street of the hamlet, Calle Darwin.

Small shops sold weird woodcarvings and tiny tortoises of black coral and bone. An old Frenchman ran the museum, a jumbled collection of shells, birds, bottled snakes and unidentifiable remains mostly collected by children, all of which smelled terrible. The small school was run by nuns, and the vital radio station sat alongside.

Brightest yellow warbler finches, and grey mockingbirds, fluttered around, while multicoloured lizards basked in the sun, unfazed by the gaggle of humans disturbing their peace.

Letter

We met the director of the Charles Darwin Research Centre who talked about the islands, and the ways they are preserving them. They've limited the passenger-carrying boats to two: our *Iguana* and a smaller one, which of course means very few people can get to the islands now, and makes me even luckier.

Back on board for another delicious lunch and more leering from the captain, now dressed in *Carry on Yachting* clothes – grey and white shorts, a too-tight jacket and Francis Chichester cap. Nothing I said could put him off.

Every morning we scrambled ashore on a different island, each entirely distinct from the last, and a treasure trove of excitement. Crowds of sea lions sunbathed as they suckled their young, watched their pups playing in rock pools, and wriggled like Marilyn Monroe in a too-tight dress down to their ankles. We swam amongst them, played with them, wary only occasionally of the bulls barking like dirty old men.

Hideous marine iguanas like corroded rusty metal clambered over each other, spitting copiously to extract salt from their bodies. The nearest relative to a dragon, they were daunting to meet face to face along the bays or in the clear blue sea.

Letter

The islands are full of the most fascinating animals. I can't adequately describe how fantastic it is swimming with sea lions who want to play with you, going right up to red-billed tropicbirds, yellow-crowned night herons, oystercatchers and albatrosses. Even the little finches and mockingbirds hop up to you, giant tortoises love you – nothing is frightened, so the harmony between creatures and humans is like nowhere else in the world. While Gordon is pretending to shoot Galápagos ducks with a stick, I wander off looking at swallow-tailed gulls, pelicans, at Sally Lightfoot crabs, at lava lizards, cacti with thick leaves and long spines, finches nesting in spiky leafless bushes, and I am incredulous and humbled. To get so close to the birds is extraordinary; watching masked boobies whistle as they mate, and blue-footed boobies dancing their courtship, passing twigs and stones to each other, while many more sit on their nests. They lay two eggs, of which only one hatches, and yet all around sit pompous, rotund, fluffy chicks. I could spend months here looking at everything, and feel unbelievably happy.

We are right on the Equator, so the sun is phenomenally strong, and I'm nut brown. Every day on a different deserted island, we have a long climb up a volcano or along cliffs, then head off to look for animals and plants. We can wander everywhere, careful not to drop our yellow camera-film boxes which lizards deem edible.

Young giant tortoises are kept in pens until big enough to fend off the rats (horrifying to see how humans can upset the balance), and the wise, ancient adults stick their necks out to be tickled.

I swam in my clothes this morning, hot after exploring another island with views over hundreds more. Sea lions were playing, grunting and splashing, while an ancient, vicious-looking bull wheezed and rasped as he and fellow bachelors lolloped at high speed up onto smooth rocks. Many display scars from battles fought. There were terrible smells of sea lion pee and dead carcasses.

Hammerhead sharks cruised around too close for comfort, and although I'm assured they never attack, they are terrifying. Another shark slid towards me, black fin up out of the water. Unfortunately he wasn't heading for the captain who had just set off fishing in a little boat.

Shearwaters flew in formation, a frigatebird caught a snake and dropped it in the sea. Pelicans with drips on their beaks zoomed in low, terns and storm petrels whizzed by. I watched in awe for hours.

Back on board, after games of chess, long talks with new-found friends, the music started, and guess who wiggled his hips and called out 'Sarita'? This was cabaret time for everyone else, who looked up from their drinks, stopped talking and waited to watch the next instalment. As he shimmied towards me, I could see Gordon smirking at the prospect of more free wine with dinner. 'Sarita, come with me tonight to visit the only other boat allowed here. We are invited. We will go after dinner.'

Dinner over, I bolted out on deck with Jacques, the troubled young Brazilian here with his family, who often explored with me and opened his heart to a foreign stranger. His long hair flew loose round a delicate, beautiful face, and I felt anxious for his future. We hid ourselves on one of the decks, and the Vermilion Flycatcher couldn't find his prey.

As dawn broke I stood on the bow while the *Iguana* motored slowly into Buccaneer Cove. Monstrous, evil-looking hammerhead sharks were drifting close by, shoals of baby ones swarmed around. I could hear, but not see, goats bleating, above a steep, sandy beach surrounded by remarkable rock formations, as if an artist had gone wild with abstract strokes of colour and shapes. After a wet landing, which meant we jumped out of our dinghy into the sea, much to the old trouts' consternation, we set off through mangroves to a lagoon where shy pintail ducks flew off in a fluster leaving thirty-five extremely pink flamingos wafting majestically in one direction, knees bending backwards, then striding in the other. Something startled them and off they went, a glorious pink group against the brilliant blues of sea and sky.

Following goat paths, we sweated uphill inland, past speckled red-legged doves pecking at tiny land crabs, savouring the heady scent of the palo santo trees beginning to bloom. Hawks hovered high in the sky, grasshoppers and bright flowers nestled into the stony ground. Every step was a wonderland.

Back on the beach, lava herons stood sculpture-still, looking like many of our fellow passengers: old men with shoulders hunched. Beautiful shells sparkled tantalisingly on pristine sand, but alas they were forbidden fruit. Profusions of seals languished on the beaches, longer fur, smaller noses, bigger eyes than sea lions. They were far quieter and friendlier and loved swimming with humans.

Another lunch, and an angry captain. 'Where were you last night? I looked for you everywhere. Now I'm off to shoot goats.' He sounded as if he wanted to shoot me too. And off he trotted. I listed the nicknames of a few passengers: Nightmare Gran, The Crab, Maurice Chevalier, Black Widow, Sparrow, Heron, Mocking Bird, Glandular Fever. Each one looked remarkably like their name. Gordon called me Rita, an abbreviation of the Vermilion Flycatcher's call.

Stopping on yet another island, we found hundreds of penguins, the second smallest in the world, shuffling around like waiters. Flightless cormorants proffered small, stump-like, unformed wings, and gaily coloured crabs scuttled sideways into dark holes. There was no fear in this world of mutual curiosity and harmony.

An ostentatious sunset competed with the colours of the day until a dignified full moon rose, casting a light of such power and other-worldliness that I was reduced to tears. A searchlight on my soul, it was an unshakeably spiritual experience.

A Canadian professor in a nose flap against the sun's rays asked Klaus, our impressively well-informed German guide, interesting questions about plants, while my young Brazilian shadow gave me a flower and followed me everywhere. Old biddies dropped out as we climbed steep volcanic slopes, reaching emerald-green lagoons, three times more saline than the sea, and looked to Cape Berkeley where the cold Humboldt Current comes through, and an invisible Equator line rings the planet. Volcanos in every direction set in a sea of pure cobalt blue.

Heat was intense, and swimming a crucial panacea, especially when seal pups were around. Just under the crystal-clear water grew a fantasy world of corals, yellow, red, green, like giant strawberries and Ascot hats.

I attempted to write letters as we sailed around, but Jacques wanted to squeeze out the last drops of his empty feelings, the full-moon tide was high under banks of mangroves, and I gave up.

Ashore, on deeply pitted lava rock, we were confronted by bull sea lions fighting, mounds of marine iguanas piled on top of each other in revolting heaps, spitting and shaking their heads. Young black Lightfoot crabs were changing to red as they aged, lizards jumped onto the backs of seal pups to catch flies, and all the time the young, mixed-up Brazilian kept pace with me.

Letter

I watch dolphins every day playing around the boat, leaping out of the clear deep water. Tuna and dorado are easily visible. This entire experience is everything a faultless world should be.

I was snorkelling one afternoon, and turned to come in when I came face to face with a hammerhead shark. Told myself to swim normally and not to splash, but my heart was pounding, and waves of pure terror must have been firing through the water. Edging closer to the shore I heard Gordon whistling, looked up, and saw the captain splashing towards me. As he put his head up, I ducked under the water and was miraculously missed by two sharks in as many minutes.

Our last night on board was a riot. Free drinks for all, a delicious dinner of fish caught by the captain, after which Hot Spot pranced in dressed as a pirate, Klaus, the guide, was dressed as Neptune in blue flippers, and they started smearing egg whites over our faces, whereupon the entire crew burst in. With huge grins they grabbed Gordon and threw him, fully clothed, into the sea. The old ladies, dressed up to the nines in shimmering old-fashioned costumes, screeched with laughter, music started, and with a lecherous wiggle from my hunter I was snared.

Gordon's wet clothes dripped in the tiny cabin, pushing humidity to breaking point, but he'd taken his ducking in good heart and given a lot of people huge pleasure, relieved it wasn't them. Luckily, Lech was inundated with passengers wanting to thank him for such a wonderful voyage, and I slipped unnoticed off the dance floor and out on deck to watch the moon transform deep shadows into white light so bright that every detail of the towering rocks was visible.

Hanging around in baking sun for several hours on a dusty landing strip with no shade, we peered hopefully into the sky until a small prop plane finally spluttered into sight. This was the only aeroplane which flew twice a week from the mainland, and took three and a half hours to cover six hundred miles. I had said genuinely sad farewells to friends made on board, ducked the captain's lunge towards my face, and suffered only a slobbering kiss and vice-like grip of my hand.

I sat on a box while we waited and sweltered, talking to the elegant Brazilian mother of Jacques and his beautiful sisters. 'Come and stay when you reach São Paulo.' Little did she know that months later I would. She had an air of vexation about her, something out of sight, but was delightfully unaffected by their obvious wealth, with ranches and houses scattered around the world.

Climbing up the wobbly makeshift aeroplane steps, I turned back for a last emotional look at paradise, with a lump in my throat, but was immediately cocooned in a small seat between Liberace looking like a walking skeleton and the gentlest doctor whose wife had recently died, who talked all the way about faith healing and Houdini.

To my surprise Moll and Kingsley's driver was waiting at the untidy cluster of huts which made up Guayaquil airport. The bus to Lima had been cancelled and wouldn't leave for another two days, which Kingsley had discovered as he microscopically checked through details I'd left with him. Unbelievably kind, they took it upon themselves to have us to stay again. And gratefully, in the bliss of air conditioning, I ate roast beef and 'Yorkshires', dodged the flying cuckoo on its kamikaze lunge every quarter of an hour, and held tightly on to a deep inner peace.

EXPLORING PERU WITH TRAINS AND TANKS

Imagine

Still in Ecuador, an overwhelmingly stinking decrepit bus rattled along a dirt road, with an equally overwhelmingly incompetent driver. We made it as far as Machala, where everyone had to pile out, grapple bags off the roof, wait, and board another antiquated jalopy to the Peruvian border. In this hot, airless sticky tin can on bald tyres, a small boy covered in scabs and sores, scratching at fleas, kept leaning over me.

Eight long hours later we reached the border from Ecuador into Peru: a confusion of shacks, police, emigration, immigration officers, money declarations. Locals shouldered lumpy cloth bags as they shuffled amongst the few foreign travellers. An Australian couple without visas were turned away, shaken and fearful, while I dragged myself and my broken case through, used now to men in uniforms armed with guns and swagger.

Our battered taxi lurched into Tumbes, a grim-looking town at the edge of the desert, whining with mosquitoes. There, Gordon and I traipsed off to the next terminal, where to my horror we discovered there were no buses to Lima for another two days, despite having booked one for that same night. For a long while I argued, pleaded, told them untruthfully a government minister was meeting us. I cried with frustration, and asked for the *jefe* (chief) to be dragged out of his house to come and sort it out – all to no avail. There was no bus leaving any time soon.

And so forty-eight grotty hours in the border town of Tumbes were spent in the rank-smelling, midge-infested Hotel Cosmos. The only loo for everyone had faeces on the floor and stank. Even the market smelled bad; flies settled on every piece of organic matter, in the corners of eyes and up nostrils of all the wretched individuals squatting motionless, unsmiling. Life was brutal.

Travelling wasn't always rose-tinted, and I couldn't begin to imagine what suffering they endured in such a godforsaken place. My peace and light-heartedness vanished, replaced with frustration and despondency, followed by a second sleepless night filled with the din of screaming men and women, broiling heat and insects with whines like sirens coming in to attack. By day the blanket humidity made me so lethargic that I slept for much of it in a dreamless heap.

Smelling as malodorous as everyone else, we eventually embarked on an ancient American Greyhound bus, long out of commission in its home country, for the one-thousand-mile drive through the desert to Lima.

Two Peruvian families wedged themselves in narrow rows behind us, impervious to the smells from their babies, rotting food, stale alcohol and unwashed clothes. They chattered merrily to each other, while I stuck to my plastic seat in competition with them as to who smelled the most revolting. In front sat an American student who had been refused entry at the border, and had taken weeks to get his documents sorted. He wanted simply now to get home. We stopped several times an hour for more passport checks, drug searches and pit stops. Each time the door opened, battalions of flies had amassed, waiting for this moment to swarm in, along with swaggering youths in police uniforms who sauntered up and down the aisle glowering accusingly at each of us.

Trujillo, where we stopped for a quick supper of tough chicken and rice, looked charming, with shaded squares and wooden balconies on whitewashed Spanish colonial houses.

Letter

It is uninterrupted desert from border to border, so for all twenty-six hours of the journey we saw nothing but sand. Mountains, dunes, plains, beaches, all solid sand. The road runs along the coast most of the way and is full of perilous hairpin bends and little hills. Lopsided overladen trucks spewing black fumes advanced towards us in the middle of the road like inebriated crabs. As the driver had his foot flat down on the accelerator, it was a pretty hairy drive, with plenty of nail-biting overtaking.

Dawn light cast shadows of blue over ridges as we peered down the dunes to the sea rolling in, and slewed to navigate sand-slides across the road. Actually we went through some nice-looking little towns full of flowers, but sadly most of the fishing villages had been reduced to piles of rubble by the October earthquake.

Lima at last, with three million inhabitants, the first impression was upliftingly encouraging. A Sheraton hotel across from the bus station gave us cool sanctuary, and a delicious lunch for £1.50, which was nonetheless a shock to the budget. As Gordon slurped furiously, we washed off the debris of two days' travelling as best we could. Then came the moment of truth as we attempted to ring precious contacts collected months ago in England, in case someone might put us up for a few nights. A Peruvian couple, Jorge and Diana Dibos, close friends of my uncle, had already offered to have me, but as usual they didn't know about Gordon.

Letter

First on the list of course were the Diboses, who knew I was coming, but disastrously, Diana explained, their daughter Nena had just left her husband after seventeen years of a miserable marriage, and had arrived to stay with her parents plus six children. So they are overflowing and unable to squeeze us in. She was incredibly apologetic and upset. I called Armando but had the wrong number. Pilar had left her house a year and a half ago. Gordon rang his contact, but she was leaving the following day. It was funny in an increasingly desperate way. As a last-ditch attempt I called the Barnetts. Mr B works for BOLSA. Their maid answered and said señora was at the airport, so a large ice cream later I tried them again, and despite having been away for a month, they immediately asked me to stay, and said they'd come right now to collect me. I hadn't mentioned Gordon, who lurked about behind pillars and potted plants when they arrived, until they realised he was somehow attached to me and said he could come too.

John is charming, tall and good-looking with a lovely sense of humour. He looks one hundred per cent English although he's one hundred per cent Chilean. Sergeant Major Monica, on the other hand, is like an extremely bossy governess, wears lace-up shoes with short white socks, has the longest blackest hairs on her legs, and has had a charm bypass. She continually interrupts. Their house is big, and could be wonderful. They have a swimming pool which we've made full use of as it's summer here and hot. For eight months of the year Lima is covered in thick fog caused by the cold Humboldt Current in the Pacific, so we're lucky to be seeing it in crisp, clear daylight. Their bouncy dog is called Pasha, and they are beyond kind to have us. Actually, I think Monica means well, but her manner is off-putting. We were greeted with the House Rules.

'You must make your beds properly, otherwise the maids feel they have to remake them.'

'You may wash your hair once a week as long as it doesn't interfere with the sightseeing programme.'

And so on.

She's the sort of person who lectures you all the time, calls him 'Daddy' and dislikes anyone to sit and read a book by themselves. We should be sightseeing twenty-four hours a day. Can't think how he puts up with her, but their two youngest boys are great characters, and drop-dead beautiful.

We have supper at seven, hours before Peruvians sit down to eat, usually jelly for pudding, which wobbles in, and it's all I can do not to hold my nose and count to three before forcing it down. Once finished, we sit round in a circle. John ties fishing flies; Sergeant M reads out loud, which makes it impossible to concentrate on anything else. I attempt to write postcards to Mexican friends, while Gordon sniffs and tries yet again to compose a letter to his mother. So far without success.

Another letter

We've now been here for a fortnight. Monica has been marvellous taking us out to Inca ruins, Indigenous villages, up into the hills, and on into the Andes up to twelve thousand feet for picnics, where we saw the famous condors cruising around high in the sky, looking more like exaggerated vultures. She's walked us along Inca trails to deserted beaches, and driven us around (the bend) residential areas of Lima, enchanting out-of-the-way corners which we'd have otherwise missed. I love this city, filled with flowers, tree-lined streets and countless parks.

Our matriarch Monica has a fascinating family history which she's only recently started telling us. Her father was a remarkable character called Charlie Milward, an incorrigible traveller, who ran away to sea when young, becoming a successful ship's captain at the beginning of the 20th century, circumnavigating the world forty-nine times, before being shipwrecked in the Strait of Magellan. As if that wasn't enough, he then embarked on disastrous financial speculations, and ended up spending his last years as the impoverished German and British consul in the far south of Chile, in Punta Arenas. And I think I'm travelling…

We've spent many hours walking until our feet are raw, round museums, galleries and churches, every day new sights and so much to learn. The Gold Museum is spectacular, a wonderful ceramics museum is filled with 8th-century erotic art, both revealing and amusing. Monica took us to an enchanting old people's home, run by a few ancient Brits who looked as if they'd been left behind by mistake. With lush gardens circling an attractive colonial house, it was a time warp from another century, where I chatted to a wizened Irish nanny, an ex-governess and an ancient, bedridden midwife. All were knitting, and so far from home. But it felt a happy place, and each of them chirped merrily like a cage of rather moth-eaten budgies.

The Dibos family have to be the nicest people anywhere. Full of charm, Jorge, the handsome father, has a divine sense of humour, Diana is glamorous and kind, immaculately dressed in crisp bright silk dresses, which make me feel like a tramp. But overwhelmingly, they are madly in love, wrapping their arms around each other, laughing at each other's jokes, which at the age of sixty is fabulous to see. He tells me that a blue whale's tongue weighs as much as an elephant, its heart as much as a car. Their pug, Pong Lee, faints when he gets overexcited, and lays turds in guests' shoes when he doesn't like them.

Walking into their house is a far cry from this one. It's filled with Peruvian treasures, ancient textiles, contemporary paintings. The entire family lives nearby, and each welcomes me with open arms as though they've known me all their lives. It's such a happy atmosphere and a wonderful insight into their privileged Peruvian life. They had vast estates and owned a bank, all of which have been taken by the military government, so of course they're apprehensive about the future. Telephones are tapped, letters opened, and people constantly, mysteriously disappear.

I've offloaded a bag of books and odd bits for Piti their son to bring to London. Please can you fish out a film in an orange Kodak box and get it developed? I'm also sending my insurance slip which needs renewing through Thomas Cook. Gordon says he can lend me money before he leaves, when we eventually reach Chile. It's horrifying how much gets eaten up by travelling and minimal day-to-day living, plus of course I buy presents for people we stay with. I've bought a record, *Jacques Loussier Plays Bach*, for the Barnetts, which is the least I can do after such an abundance of generosity. Must stop now, just waiting for marching orders from Major Monica.

Later letter

Hopefully by now BOLSA in London will have given you the telex message that we're OK, despite the horrible situation here in Lima. The police went on strike against the military junta and were given until midnight to return to work. They refused, so the army surrounded their headquarters with tanks, set fire to it, and 180 policemen were killed. I heard the noise going on all night, shooting, machine-gun fire, tanks and helicopters. The Correo paper factory burnt to the ground (we could see the clouds of smoke), and next morning was chaos: more buildings on fire, random shooting and horrendous looting by people from the slums on the outskirts, who, with no police to stop them, went berserk, ripping buildings apart. The most effective tactic the army could dream up was to send helicopters to fire on the crowds and simply mow them down. A curfew was imposed and anyone out is shot on sight.

This nightmare was apparently started when a minister in the Revolutionary Government of the Armed Forces, a general, slapped a traffic cop in the face when he wasn't allowed to queue-barge past in his car. This was seen by other cops who tried to force the minister to apologise, which he wouldn't. Violence kicked off, martial law was declared, night-time curfew, no talking in groups, and all news bulletins silenced, so no one knew what was going on.

I walked to the Dibos family enclave where Jorge arrived from work having seen tanks chewing up the main roads, soldiers shooting in the air to stop looters, bayonets fixed and used. Military planes flew over and rumours ran riot. By the time I walked back to Casa Barnett, queues had already stretched outside the bakery for bread, and cars formed long lines for petrol. Trucks lined the residential streets, hundreds of them parked for the night, unable to move during the curfew.

That evening we settled down as usual. I tried not to listen to Monica reading out loud, but it was impossible for any of us to concentrate, so we handed cups of coffee to the soldiers outside, who cocked their rifles, shooting at shadows, full of stories of trouble in the centre of town.

Each day troops patrolled the streets, most of them in their teens, nervous, with orders to fire on anyone disobeying the new rules. The Reuters correspondent was kicked out of the country, so no news would filter out, and we fed ourselves on rumour. The newspapers were full of propaganda, and the wireless blasted out pro-military-regime programmes. Mobs ransacked and vandalised with impunity, torching whatever would burn. Each night I was woken by shots ringing out, by tanks rumbling past, and by the soldiers on patrol clicking their guns right outside my window. Most of them were as frightened as everyone else, and so nervy they let off their guns immediately anything made them jump.

Letter

It's shocking to see the generals having such power. Soak the rich, but don't give to the poor. Put in the uniform pocket and use it to corrupt. Peru is filled with Russians. Communism to the fore. There are rumours the CIA is also involved. Who knows, it's chaos.

Yesterday we were in the centre, walking miles as always, round museums and churches, surprisingly still open, when shooting broke out as we walked out of the cathedral. The square was surrounded by tanks, guns swinging round ready to fire, so we dived across to the Sheraton, conveniently there for us, and bumped into Milu, a glamorous Brazilian woman who'd been on our Galápagos trip, and spent hours hiding in the hotel until the coast was clear, by which time she'd invited me to stay in her house in Rio when I eventually get there. She has a house at Ipanema (remember that song, 'The Girl From Ipanema'?)

Days passed in a medley of more catacombs, convents, private collections, pre-Inca pottery, gold, silver and mummies. Almost every collection had an erotic section of ancient pottery, showing men with much to brag about, women with letter boxes, couples in every conceivable and inconceivable position. There were men with animals, gay couples and intimate kissing. They had a good time all those years ago.

One evening after dinner, Monica played the piano, badly, and then fell asleep, so I was able to finish Graham Greene's *The Honorary Consul* in relative peace, until the telephone rang, and John was informed there would be serious trouble the next day, that we must keep away from the centre. We could already hear machine-gun fire, and single shots breaking the silence of the curfew. The Dibos family were quietly making plans to flee to Costa Rica.

Days filled with even more bizarre exploring, passing burnt-out shops, to palaces with ornate gilt decoration, bulbous balconies and manicured formal gardens. We reached them along narrow side tracks, edges of fields, keeping off main roads blockaded with protestors from all sides of the political spectrum. Lima had an overdose of spectacularly grandiose buildings, stuffed with fabulous treasures. Too much to take in, and although suffering from art indigestion, I still continued sightseeing , often diverted by sudden shooting into the peace of an unvisited church, or into the depths of a basement, or up into a random office block.

One Sunday, John and Monica packed their camper van with food and drink, with faded towels and beach balls, and eight of us squeezed in, to set off for a day at the seaside. Gordon and me, the two beautiful boys David and Peter, Hairy Legs and John, plus two cousins. It felt like an outing in 1950s England. We parked on the beach, erected a large stripy awning, and settled down like a scene from H. E. Bates. The sea was Humboldt Current cold, large waves battered our bodies as they unfurled onto the white sand, and kept us shrieking, warm and tingling. We half-heartedly chucked balls at each other, cooked delicious kingfish, bought from the fisherman, over an open fire, and were about to go for a walk along the beach when orders came to pack everything up and drive the two hours back into Lima. Monica was feeling 'nauseated'. Whether it was due to her fellow passengers or the food, none of us knew, but it felt strange to step back into a battle zone again, as if the entire day had vanished into an old-fashioned dream. We wondered what would happen next.

In Lima, little happened as far as I was aware: earthquake damage from the previous months blended in with the new destruction of recent days. Surfers continued to ride the waves, soldiers crowded squares, and new recruits, or were they prisoners, marched through the streets. The silence of night-time curfews was broken with gunfire, helicopters and booming tanks. It didn't seem real.

But gradually, the days felt safer, and it was time to move on, south towards Bolivia. To leave the comfort and generosity of all those who had looked after us, taken us in and selflessly shared their way of life with us.

Gordon didn't speak a syllable of Spanish, his attempt at 'see you later' was '*hasta l'huevo*' (see you egg), so arranging tickets was left to me. First we needed to obtain a tourist card from the Bolivian Consulate, then to change money legally in a bank with appalling rate of exchange. While we hung around, an annoying woman sighed and typed slowly with one finger, stamping and signing never-ending pieces of paper. On to the Tepsa bus terminal where I queued for what felt like a week, chatting to a nice Italian going our way. And still we scoured Spanish colonial Lima; into the Convent of San Francisco with cloisters tiled from Seville, wooden balcony from Nicaragua and Zurbarán paintings of the apostles.

Our sergeant major stopped feeling nauseated and insisted on showing us the Inquisition rooms, handsome carved wooden ceilings giving way to gruesome torture chambers, which could probably have been put back into use once more. It was eerie, and I persuaded the guard to let me use the crackly telephone in his little hut to ring Diana Dibos. 'Meet you in the Sheraton for lunch,' she laughed. So, making excuses, I left our military commander and headed for that well-known landmark. There was sexy Brazilian Milu again with her little daughters, who joined us, and listened as Diana explained how her first husband had been shot. At that moment shooting and looting flared up in the sunlight outside, shops closed down and fire extinguishers were dragged across marble floors. We had to stay there for a long while until it seemed quiet again, and I could creep out and wait until the buses started up, to catch one back to my base in the leafy residential suburb.

Meanwhile Gordon had been wandering: 'Found a long-haired young fellow playing the lute.' I sighed, he was only twenty-four, with the vocabulary of an old man.

I had fallen for one of the Dibos sons with dreamy dark bedroom eyes and thought-provoking questions. I loved being amongst them, and despite all that was happening, their houses were filled with laughter, relaxed sophistication, cosmopolitan views. I had a lump in my throat when we said goodbye. Once more I'd felt completely loved.

I had grown extremely fond of the Barnetts too. They hadn't deserved my sarcasm, but had put up with us for weeks, and looked after us beautifully. Monica had shown us every corner of Lima and beyond, and when we said goodbye, she suddenly melted, tears running down her face, as she handed over a large bag of food for the journey, thoughtfully chosen nuts, bread, cheese and fruit.

I nipped round to the side of the bus and squatted out of the glare of headlights to have a pee before a final hug goodbye.

And off we rattled through the night towards Arequipa, inching closer to Bolivia, and therefore Chile.

Sometime in the middle of the night I was woken from my head-lolling doze to see the barrel of a tank gun facing down the bus. The driver climbed down gesticulating, and after much arguing and producing of documents, we were allowed to continue our twenty-four-hour marathon. The curfew was being rigorously imposed. Again and again we were stopped, and all foreigners on board had to get out for police checks. Cockroaches scuttled along the filthy floor, and I dreaded the exhaustion of a hot day ahead.

As the sun's rays cleared the dark of night, dramatic desert scenery was revealed, punctuated with lush valleys, lonely adobe houses hidden amongst silvery-green poplar trees. And eventually, late in the evening, we reached Arequipa, where to our total surprise, as we staggered to the ground, we were met by an Indian chauffeur called Jespar. He drove us to a wonderfully eccentric old house, lived in by a charming elderly Peruvian couple who'd been telephoned by Jorge Dibos in Lima, and asked to look after us. Don Alberto Llaso, small, balding and the sweetest man, plied us with presents before sending us off to the Presidente Hotel.

Letter

He paid for us to stay in the best hotel in Arequipa. Firmly insisted, and thus we had two unexpected days of blissful luxury, able to wash clothes and ourselves in anticipation of the coming days.

Unbelievably generous. We were also lent their car and driver, who took us around the Spanish colonial town, neat and compact rather like Antigua, the old capital of Guatemala. It sits on the border where desert meets green grass, fertile valleys and mountains, and feels like a frontier into another world.

There's a marvellous convent complex, Santa Catalina, in the centre, which until recently was a closed order, but has now opened to the public as there are only thirty-two of the Dominican nuns left. An immense area of pretty coloured houses, cloisters, orange trees and fountains, but the atmosphere was sad. Along cobbled streets, squeaky clean under the harsh glare of the sun, many of the churches are built of white lava. It's a gem.

Jespar drove us out into the countryside, past fluffy white llamas, and shaggy alpacas, willow trees, cows and bowler-hatted Indigenous women, but I was so sleepy I could barely speak, let alone take in new smells and sights as we swung around in the back of the car.

I stocked up in a gaudy market with figs, fruit and cheese for the evening train to Cuzco, and read in the hotel café as rain belted down, making rivers of cobbled lanes. Before he took us to the station, Jespar brought Don Alberto and his endearing half-English wife, Alice, round to say goodbye. They've lived here for fifty years, and she has never been to Cuzco.

Rain still torrential; the rainy season has started in the mountains, and it really buckets down. The poor driver tore along the platform trying, without success, to find us a space in the train where we could perch. Every carriage was completely packed.

We had bought first-class tickets – the difference of sitting on a hard-backed chair, as opposed to second-class wooden bench, and had arrived at the station two hours before the train left, but it was already crammed to the roof with colourful locals, scratching their heads, with their distinctive smell of unwashed bodies and slept-in clothes. I managed to squeeze onto half a second-class seat next to two Colombians, who let me huddle under their rugs. They were making a pilgrimage to Machu Picchu; Roberto, tall and spiritual, discussed belief systems, while Daniel sported a woolly hat with side flaps, so, he told me, the condors wouldn't find him. Dominic, a thin, tired Frenchman, tagged along. They were friendly and kind, but none of us had any sleep. Damp turned to freezing cold as the train climbed steadily, and soon we were puffing through deep snow and icy winds. Gordon was squished in somewhere I couldn't see him, while all around hundreds of bowler-hatted women covered the floor, snoring happily. These hats were introduced by British railway workers in the 1920s, taken up and worn by Quechua and Aymara women ever since.

Sometime in the night, two Indigenous women started fighting over a hat, and were silently pulling each other's hair out, while the rest lay or sat in their huge, full skirts, wrapped in ponchos, fast asleep. The whole scene was reminiscent of being in a movie, even the train in *Doctor Zhivago* broke into my thoughts as I scrutinised intriguing, worn faces, wondering what stories these people might tell.

The nauseating stink of the loo filtered through the carriage and a small girl was sick over the floor by my feet.

I didn't exactly wake up as I hadn't slept. Another dawn revealed an entirely different country to the one we'd left in the half-light of an Arequipa evening. Spectacular snow-covered mountains dominated the horizon, green hills looming over us were criss-crossed with ancient Inca terracing, the sky, petrol-blue stormy, released torrents of rain. We passed herds of llamas and alpacas, watched over by barefoot women whose small, muddy, dirty villages sat miserably beside potholed tracks. Everywhere reeked of poverty-tough lives.

My stomach was bloated, jeans too tight, and the pain, as well as exhaustion, competed for attention with the grandeur of the scenery sliding past, until the train shuddered to a random halt, and we all stumbled out to wash hands and faces in hot, bubbling streams from thermal springs, catapulting inertia into space.

As we chugged on past rivers raging in flood, silver-leafed eucalyptus plantations appeared, neater villages gradually changed to rustic tiled roofs, and at every halt children leapt aboard selling alpaca slippers, and rugs the colours of autumn. It was cold, wild, beautiful, and hard to stay awake, but it was very much the Peru I had imagined.

Letter

Cuzco, the old capital of the Incas, reminds me of Salamanca. It's a beautiful colonial town, with small green parks, cobbled streets and pretty churches. Surrounded on all sides by green hills, it's softly coloured and postcard picturesque.

Our *pensión* has great wooden beds, but bathrooms that are so disgusting I can't face a shower. Faeces all over the floor. You can imagine the smell.

Having haggled over the price of our room, Gordon and I set off into the heart of Cuzco, the beautiful floodlit Plaza de Armas bustling with students. Happy and relieved to be on my feet, I farted my way along streets filled with ruddy-cheeked Quechuans, barefoot, friendly, sporting hats with ear flaps and nattering with each other in their local dialect. Market stalls were stocked with lust-worthy, rough home-knitted ponchos, gloves and socks. Alas, I had no room in my already bulging and broken red case, nor confidence in my fragile finances. But I trawled the crude stands, hopping over deep puddles, dodging rain as it poured off makeshift tarpaulins.

We queued a long while at the railway station to buy tickets for the journey to Puno and Machu Picchu, excited that the next small stage of the journey was fixed, and by four the following morning, we were back on the platform struggling with crowds of sharp-elbowed Indigenous locals to board the train.

Letter

We managed to thrust our way into a little mountain train with a gleaming black steam engine, and set off for Machu Picchu, the ancient sacred city of the Incas. As we wove our way through ever-more impressive country, the snow-capped mountains grew larger, the Urubamba River, in full flood, catapulted down over vast boulders, like thick chocolate, and banks of wild orchids, gladioli and lupins carpeted the ground.

The train stopped briefly at Aguas Calientes, a row of little shacks along the railway line, where I raced out to a peeling green tin hut and booked beds in a dormitory for the night. Tearing back I clung on to the train as it pulled out and steamed on to the Machu Picchu halt, where again it was a race to get onto the back of the only truck going up the mountain, grinding around terrifying bends, the track zigzagging ever higher. Tangles of wildflowers concealed the ground with vibrant colour, and views for which there were no superlatives shimmered in the heat of the sun.

With a judder and severe jolt, we reached the summit, and there they were: the ruins I had been longing to see, rediscovered in 1911, impressive and very much intact, each piece of geometric, cleverly cut stone slotted together like a jigsaw puzzle. From this height the river looked miles below, while green mountains surrounded us, tinged with purples and soft blues. I sat for hours on a perfect Inca-cut rock, absorbing an ethereal sense of other-worldliness, until Gordon wandered over suggesting we should climb Huayna Picchu, a steep, narrow thumb of a mountain thrusting even higher into the hot blue sky. The tiny track was vertical and slippery, but we made it up to the pointed summit, where boundless views rewarded breathless effort. Breathtaking in every way. As we gazed down on to the ruins of Machu Picchu way below, we perched on boulders, sharing bread and cheese from the bakery in Cuzco with Bill, a rangy American who had useful tips for Bolivia. The train and station looked like tiny toy sets on another world.

Letter

There's only one small and very expensive hotel by the ruins, so we slithered all the way down Huayna Picchu, had the best, most extravagant can of Coke in my life. Better than champagne. Then walked the entire way down the main mountain, via little short-cut paths, picking flowers, stopping by streams and waterfalls, crossing the raging, foaming river, so noisy that the silence afterwards rang in my ears. Eventually we reached the railway line. There are no roads at all in the valley. It had started raining drops the size of birds' eggs, so there was nothing for it but to walk along the track towards our shelter for the night, through long, dripping inky-dark tunnels, hopping over puddles. Of course we were completely drenched. Eventually the straggle of shacks that is Aguas Calientes came into view, and we found our dormitory, sharing it with a bunch of Chilean students, a Scotsman, Brazilians and a New Zealander. There was no light anywhere, unless someone lit a match, one outside tap sufficed for all of us, but I simply fell onto the grubby, damp sheets of a bottom bunk and passed out.

All ten of us seemed to wake at the same time in the predawn dark, and gradually struggled out of soggy beds, groped for our clothes, and took turns to brush teeth from the single tap outside while rain poured down on us. We sat beside the track under a shelter, munching *choclos*, the staple and delicious corn on the cob cooked over an open fire by poncho-wearing women, on sale wherever there's a travellers' halt.

When the steam train, puffing clouds of smoke and hooting furiously, came close, we jumped on to the side, clutching anything that would hold us. I had one foot on a large screw and only just made it, until the guard came along and hauled me onto firmer footing. We were heading back to the Machu Picchu stop, unaware that there had been a heavy landslide during the night and most of the track up ahead had been washed away.

Letter

Again, we raced to climb onto the back of a truck, but after a short while of grinding gears and skidding dangerously close to the edges, we were turfed off, and had to walk up the rest of the way, climbing over boulders in the drizzle. It's miles, took hours, but was so worthwhile, as mists swirled through the mountains, transforming the world into a dream. We had the entire ancient city to ourselves, possibly the most beautiful peaceful place I have ever seen. Another deeply moving experience.

Journal

On the four-hour train ride back to Cuzco, I sat opposite a smiling woman who sold fruit in the market, along with her young son, Bocho, and a dirty, grinning little girl. We giggled and played catch with lemons, Bocho and his sister grovelling on the filthy floor, playing in the unspeakable loo, returning to nag their mother for a maize stick to chew. I spotted my favourite cloth bag, lost the previous night, being clutched by a Brazilian couple who refused to give it back. Strange to see it again being used by someone else. I saw the Weeza Man (the German from San José) and others from Cuzco, everyone friendly, exchanging travel tips, surrounded by crowds of local women in mad-hatter top hats. An especially beautiful girl wearing a white one stood out from the rest, and outside, as the sun came through, everything felt happy and alive.

Mountains in their cloaks of blue-grey and purples posed, as always, statuesque against racing clouds and a brilliant sky.

Back in Cuzco the days were hot, the nights crispy cold, and I was so stiff from clambering around Machu Picchu that I could barely walk. But restaurants serving pisco sours and lasagne, ice creams and filled avocados gradually restored equilibrium. The little *pensión* was filled with Brazilians, who sang and chatted late into the nights, Trini Lopez and 'La Bamba' reverberated through flimsy walls. I wanted, as so often, to freeze the moment and stay a while.

An ancient local bus with rusty seats, mostly unattached to the floor, rumbled along unpaved roads through the Urubamba valley. Small green fields were lined with ubiquitous eucalyptus, willows and poplars, backed by high green mountains, now fantastically terraced. We crossed a small wooden bridge over the smooth, fast-flowing river, and arrived in Pisac, a tiny, scruffy village with immense charm. Munching on sweet, juicy, freshly cooked *choclos*, I explored the cobbled, narrow streets filled with Quechua coming to market. No foreigners around as I sat in the square, watching barefoot men in muddy white baggy trousers with embroidered tunics, wandering together, while women in wonderful beaded ear-flap hats and familiar top hats set up their stalls. They sold roughly made beads of clay from the river as they chewed dried coca leaves, the ever-present crop that has been grown in South America for over eight thousand years. It's a crucial crutch for the Indigenous people as a stimulant to numb their constant hunger and exhaustion. Rich in nutrients, and especially helpful against altitude sickness, and stomach problems, most locals carry pouches filled with leaves dangling from their waistbands.

Letter

Travelling on, always moving, always saying goodbye.

New sights and smells, new sensations. Breathing new air keeps adrenaline pumping, and anticipation on high alert.

Many times each day I unfolded my crucial companion, a large map of Central and South America, plotting routes, working out days ahead. The fold lines were worn, and towns written across them became impossible to decipher. But now we needed to edge south towards Chile, and decided to go by train to Juliaca, and on to the shores of Lake Titicaca in Bolivia. Not to be outdone this time, we arrived at Cuzco's station, climbed over a wall to reach the platform, four hours before the train was due to leave. It was already heaving, and as the train shunted in, Gordon tore up and down, leapt aboard, and commandeered two seats while I sat on our bags to guard them. People were shouting, shoving, fighting. Mayhem, impossible to reserve anything in advance, anticipation of each train journey caused restless nights. But we were on, had something to sit on, and dozed as we trundled on our way, while a white bright moon flooded the countryside like an eerie spotlight.

Letter

From Juliaca we bundled into a *collectivo*, or shared, taxi to Puno, a drab little village on the shores of the lake, where we found a foul room, dumped our bags and set off to find a boat to visit the floating islands of the Uros Indians. Lake Titicaca is the highest navigable lake in the world, and the altitude gives its colours a startling clear luminosity, entirely unlike anything I've seen before.

We bartered a long while about price with a chubby old captain, who eventually took us out in his decrepit boat through channels of yellow reeds, passing men in reed boats collecting reeds. The water was deep blue-green and raw cold.

The Uros live in windowless miniature reed huts, planted with a squelch on floating islands built of reeds from totora plants. They even manage to eat their reeds. It's an odd spongy sensation to pick one's way around the islands, and I can't imagine how they survive, with almost no clothes, at such a great height. Few of them have ever touched dry land. Women sit on soggy reeds weaving extremely primitive strips of cloth, or feeding children, while men fish for salmon from little reed boats, shooting flamingos and other exotic birds for meat. It's fascinating to watch them. I wish you could see the lake yourselves, it's so hard to describe the colours, and at this altitude there's nothing to compare them with. Stunningly beautiful. One of the islands boasted a school hut, where I spoke to a dedicated, gentle young Spanish-speaking Adventist teacher. He must have an isolated life floating around amongst people who speak only Aymara.

Covered in oil from our boat, I eventually found the office, hidden by smoke, for the old British tramp steamer, built in 1862, and launched on the lake, after many delays, in 1870. She had been carried by mules up to this altitude of almost four thousand metres, for 220 miles, and was still one of only a few ships on the lake. The *Yavari* had been designed for the Peruvian Navy, as part cargo, passenger, gunboat, and was fuelled for many years with dried llama dung. On Wednesdays, she made the eleven-hour crossing to Guaqui in Bolivia, carrying up to eighty passengers, and here there were at least three times that number of people trying to book a ticket on the next voyage, so no chance for us. It suddenly seemed as if every traveller was taking our route. The only bus had broken down, and any *collectivo* taxis, those that squashed as many people into them as possible, were fully booked for days.

Letter

As you can imagine, we were desperate, there didn't seem any way out at all, and Puno was alright for a day, but no more. Gordon and I tried everything and everyone, tramping the muddy streets, queuing at every taxi, lorry, bus. It just wasn't possible. All the time there were other travellers pushing and shoving, trying to get out too. We met up with the Brazilians from Cuzco who'd had no luck either. Travelling in South America isn't like anywhere else; there are very few roads, mostly unpaved, all unreliable and much of the time the only form of transport is to hitch a ride on a lorry taking cattle to market – if you're lucky.

Eventually we gave up trying, utterly exhausted, dreaming of another world, and went back to our little room. A few moments later a man burst in saying there were two spaces in a mini truck going to the border. The eight-hour journey would cost £2 each. We grabbed our cases and raced to it, squeezed in amongst twenty others and set off for the Bolivian border around Lake Titicaca on the worst track I'd yet seen. Full of potholes, deeply rucked mud, we drove through churning rivers and skidded precariously. Luckily, fellow travellers were charming; some older Argentinians, Brazilian students with guitars, and young Peruvians who chatted happily as we rocked and rattled along the altiplano at 12,500 feet, watching women and girls in heavily padded skirts, spinning yarn and weaving as they minded sheep, alpacas and llamas. We passed hundreds of tiny stone-walled fields, each growing potatoes, staple crop of the country, with miniscule adobe and reed huts, sharply defined in the intense clarity of high-altitude colours and light.

Letter

Despite the acute discomfort, I wouldn't have missed the journey for the world. Eventually, at dusk, we arrived at the border, which consists of a few isolated semi-derelict sheds, to find it was just closing. We managed to race through the notoriously tricky Peruvian side with no trouble, as the customs officers were longing to get home, and staggered on, over the only bridge, on foot, to find the Bolivians had already packed up and gone. So we split up, and set off to find the immigration officer, who stamps passports, hauled him out of his house and bribed him to come back to his office and let us through. Extremely unwilling, he eventually ambled up to a shed, to find he'd locked it and left the key inside. Pulling his gun out, he smashed a window with the butt, and climbed through jagged glass, crunching shards under his heavy boots as he searched for a Bolivian stamp in the rubbish-strewn chaos over which he presided. A long while later we were once more on our way, by which time we'd also had to bribe the driver of the last bus going to La Paz to wait for us, otherwise we would be stuck in the sub-zero altitude of now 13,000 feet with no shelter.

ON TOP OF THE WORLD WITH FEMALE SMUGGLERS IN BOLIVIA

River Deep – Mountain High

A dramatic sunset spread across Lake Titicaca, throwing wispy slivers of reflections from the sky into the surprisingly responsive water. Darkness fell fast, surrounded us, and off we lurched, half the bus filled with foreign travellers on one side, the other with amusing Indigenous women smuggling contraband across the border. They had drugs, jerseys, Dralon shirts, nylon pyjamas stuffed into their voluminous multitude of petticoats. They wore varieties of their ubiquitous bowlers, nothing which might have kept them warm, and gossiped ferociously as we all bounced slowly towards La Paz, administrative capital of Bolivia.

We stopped at several checkpoints, where scruffy police armed with pistols, looking as if they slept in their uniforms, came aboard to search the women. Each time a few of them were hauled off, protesting, and stripped of their packages, although as soon as the bribe was paid, they padded up again. Corruption was so blatant it was funny, but it was also getting colder and colder. Most of the windowpanes were missing, and those that were more or less intact were riven with cracks creating draughts that seemed to penetrate every bone in our stiff bodies.

We all had to get out at some of the makeshift barriers and give our passports to the police, which necessitated another long wait while the smuggling women stripped each other and rearranged their black-market goods.

Alicia, who possessed only two top teeth, was the life and soul of the party, giggling at everything, in particular at Gordon when he said '*no, gracias*' in an especially English voice, in reply to her offer of buying a jersey. She had a doll-like daughter called Betty, dressed in the same grubby petticoats, fringed homespun poncho and battered hat. Clearly a foil for the smuggling gang, she gazed innocently at each of us, daring us to challenge her.

We rocked, rolled and splashed in beetle-black darkness through almost continuous floodwater, and precariously through thundering rivers, when suddenly, at around midnight, we came to a huge torrent of a river which had broken its banks. There was absolutely no way we could cross. By the feeble headlight – our bus had only one which worked – we could make out a lorry stuck in the middle, being pushed around by the water like a child's toy. There was nothing we could do to help, and we later heard that the bus before ours had been swept away.

Letter

So we had to stay there for the night, at an altitude of almost thirteen thousand feet, to wait for the water to subside. I can't tell you how cold and uncomfortable it was. Zero legroom, knees squashed against the back of the seat in front, with so many broken windows we might have been outside, howling draughts – I didn't doze for one second. Meanwhile the well-practised *contrabandistas* immediately slept, snored and farted, padded by their illicit wares, oblivious to their surroundings.

Then Gordon passed out, numb with cold and lack of air at that altitude. There was little space on his seat, he was bent forwards and found it hard to breathe. Luckily the Argentinians were in front and helped me drag him outside, where we all slapped his face to revive him, although I'm not sure that's a recommended cure. They miraculously produced an almost empty bottle of whisky, the remains of which we managed to pour down his throat. Toothless Alicia shuffled out and stuffed a coca leaf in his mouth, and thyme-like herbs up his nose. We pushed and pulled him back onto the bus and he was soon sleeping as well as the locals, while I remained doubled up, stupefied with cold.

At first light, the waters had slightly subsided, and our driver decided to have a go at crossing. We hesitated on the edge, rocked precariously, wheels whirred as we held our collective breath, and managed somehow to churn through the raging water and up onto the other side. I was like a block of ice, so stiff I couldn't move.

High in the dramatic altiplano, snow on the Andean mountains and volcanos, there were more police checks, more bribing, scuffling and hiding packages, as we struggled to navigate the appalling main route from Peru into Bolivia. Did you know that Bolivia is twice the size of Spain and has only one tarmac road from La Paz, the capital, to another town?

At long last we came over the brow of a hill and there, suddenly, unexpectedly, lay the incredible sight of La Paz in a huge basin below, the highest capital in the world.

We wound our way deep down the rutted road into the centre, saying sad farewells to our kind Argentinian friends, grateful to have arrived. Before long a drab room in a gloomy hotel seemed like paradise. It had a tepid shower, not just cold water, under which I scrubbed days of grime out of my hair, body and clothes, and felt reborn, except that I hadn't slept for thirty-six hours.

A poster of Raquel Welch and Paul Newman pouted at us from the wall, mocking the decrepitude below.

La Paz surprised me more than any other city thus far. I had imagined a drab little town with muddy streets and corrugated iron roofs. Instead, it was full of charm, cobbled streets, colonial buildings, bustling with character, good shops, even a few high-rise blocks. It felt cosmopolitan, like an oasis in the middle of an untouched moonscape. The notorious prison, San Pedro, where wives and children of convicted inmates shared their cells, and left for work and school through the front gates each day, was surprisingly in the heart of the city. The enormous old building lined one side of the quiet Plaza San Pedro, where ubiquitous *choclo* sellers were doing a roaring trade with men and women waiting to visit, while in the narrow streets around there was no sign of police or armed guards.

Gordon was getting me down. He was so bloody English, his slurping was driving me insane, and he seemed never to notice his surroundings. He took an age to understand what was going on, hadn't picked up a word of Spanish, and was embarrassed at sharing a room with me. 'Blooming heck,' he muttered, as he tried to wrap a towel around his middle to undress, and desperately grabbed at it when it inevitably fell to the floor. He usually finished taking his clothes off under the bedclothes.

I should have felt mean, but took great pleasure in giving him the slip, zipping onto buses, letting him find a seat amongst breastfeeding women with several small, grubby children attached to them. He was leaving when we reached Chile, which wouldn't be a moment too soon, but now in La Paz we queued in the First National City Bank for several hours, and eventually he was able to lend me the enormous sum of three hundred dollars, to last for the rest of my journey. A fortune, for which I was immensely grateful. The jovial Bolivian bank manager spent an inordinate amount of time working out this transaction, explaining intricacies of the currency black market in Chile and Argentina. Corruption seemed to be a way of life everywhere we went.

We found the British Embassy, where a letter from my mother was waiting; trying to be upbeat, she admitted that she and my father would eventually part company. I felt sick; although I had seen this coming for a long while, it had never been specifically clarified. She told me they would sell the house I had begun to think of as a possible home – the first one in England, and she would eventually go and live with her new man. Where was my father? He was seldom mentioned, nor did he ever write to me, so I worried for his loneliness, and wondered where he was living. It made me dread going back.

I left a message for the British ambassador, H. E. Hope-Jones, to whom I had a vague introduction, and after reading a few ancient copies of *The Times*, Gordon and I tramped off to have our passports stamped with a visa for Chile. The man in the consul office shut the door in our faces. 'No good here office,' he yelled, and after being frisked at the immigration department, we discovered that was also the wrong place, so gave up and explored the Witches' Market: stalls filled with llama foetuses, skulls, evil-smelling potions, dried who-knew-what.

Letter

Mr Hope-Jones collected us in his two-ton armour-plated Austin Princess with buttons and alarms for demobilising, an armed guard along with the chauffeur, and Mrs Hope-Jones, his easy-going, giggly, somewhat scatty wife, who loathes having to trail round the predictably stultifying diplomatic cocktail parties. Their rather sad-looking daughter is also here, aged twenty-four, and is her mother's social secretary. They were taking us to the highest ski resort in the world, Chacaltaya, with one cronky lift at eighteen thousand feet up in the Andes. A beautiful drive past llamas, alpacas, winding up the mountains until we left the treeline behind, then the grass, and eventually we were in deep, glistening snow. I was hoping to ski, but at that altitude would have probably fallen flat on my face, so walked slowly, gasping for breath, spaniels Smog and Tweedie oblivious to the thin air, bouncing around in the snow. We wolfed down a delicious picnic, sitting on the bonnet of their car, so now my face is like a lobster it's so burnt, even after such a short time. H. E. smokes a pipe, puffing and sucking, always a marksman bodyguard shadowing him.

From that dizzy height we descended, right down into the Zongo Valley, past magnificent lakes of greens and greys, riots of wildflowers, flocks of birds floating on the thermals, and the always astounding scenery. The country, the altiplano as it's called, is barren, but hauntingly beautiful with mysterious shadows, and tones melding into each other like liquid paint. Far lovelier than I'd ever imagined. We passed a sad little tin-mining village with a cemetery looking forlorn. Silver and tin are still mined over a huge part of the country by Indigenous men, for large, often foreign, companies, and stories of horrendous accidents are told everywhere we stop. No safety measures or doctors in situ, and no rural hospitals. As they describe their miserable lives, the men look at me and say it's unlucky for a woman to go down a mine.

They have their demon god, Tio, who, they believe, protects them as they work deep underground, whose statues, with goat hooves, man's body and fearsome horned animal head, reside in the depths of each mine. Underneath the mountains, precarious with their insides hollowed out, miners start each shift by praying, and offering Tio sacrifices in exchange for their lives. Usually cigarettes and alcohol are proffered, although rumours abound of babies and unconscious drunks being dumped, and abandoned as offerings to assuage his terrifying hunger. It's a creepy thought.

We stopped at the foot of the Huayna Potosí mountain, its 21,000 feet silhouetted against the brightest cobalt sky, and saw Lake Titicaca in the distance, wonderful bleak blue mountains for ever.

Back to tea with crumpets and cakes at the Residence, where I sat in comfort on the loo, and gazed longingly at the bath. It was a large, cosy house and rather unsettled me. I felt a twinge of longing to stay somewhere like this for a while, and to sleep in a comfortable bed. Perhaps a little homesick for a home I would no longer have.

Wandering around La Paz, exploring museums filled with pots, shrunken heads, skulls exposing brain operations, beads of teeth, I passed a crowd of young, shaven-headed army, air force and even naval troops (Bolivia lost its Pacific coastline to Chile in 1879), strutting along the steep cobbles with their girlfriends, white gloved, saluting each other. Smart.

The church of San Franciso had a funeral in full swing, packed with mourners in black, while a young priest in purple stood out from the crowd looking theatrical against the magenta altar cloth.

Then I found the black market, on the steepest cobbled back street, where all our Peruvian fellow bus passengers took their illicit wares to barter and sell. I looked in vain for toothless Alicia and baby Betty, but no doubt they were back on another bus struggling once more across the border, padded with smuggled contraband.

Carolyn Hope-Jones Junior turned up at our hotel to take Gordon and me to the cinema. What luxury and culture. *The Secret of Santa Vittoria* with Anthony Quinn and Virna Lisi was playing, and of course I fell in love with AQ. Before it started, there was a hilarious and overlong advertisement for Tampax, which felt incongruous, given the majority of the female population would be unlikely to have access to anything like that. There were plenty of areas in La Paz alone where sanitation was an open sewer, and most houses and huts had no more than a hole in the ground.

Letter

Sadly, because it's the rainy season, we can't get out to any other places, as the so-called roads have been washed away, and more of the rivers have overflowed. I'm not risking another journey like the last one, although now it's over I wouldn't have missed it for anything. Every day I'm blown away by the glorious views of the Illimani mountain towering over La Paz, the staggering colours. Of all the countries I've touched so far, this is the one I can't wait to come back to and explore.

Journal

Five and a half months today on the road. Scrambled off early into the cold of La Paz and managed to board the marvellous old British train built in 1880, filled with freshly polished brass, gaslights and huge black leather armchairs. Small carriages lined with mahogany carried locals in anoraks, stripy ponchos and large loads, while out of the old-fashioned windows we watched the endlessly fascinating sights of Indigenous women watching over their herds of llamas and alpacas, wild vicuñas grazing nearby, as we chugged slowly south towards the north of Chile. We spluttered painfully, slowly, up hills, hitched more carriages, and bumbled on and on and on through rainstorms across the altiplano.

Letter

Even the smallest child who can barely walk is dressed as a mini mirror image of its parents. We passed poor little villages, windowless shacks built of grass mixed with mud and llama droppings, beside wildly raging rivers. Llamas, who live off the toughest grasses to keep their teeth from growing too long, are vital pack animals, their meat and wool important for protein and ponchos. They're pregnant for eleven months, but can give birth each year, a kind of miracle animal. I remember Monica in Peru tutting over the pronunciation of llama. 'It's "yama"', she would say, 'a lama's a Tibetan monk.' It's an intriguing country from another century, ravaged by Spaniards, now plundered for minerals by others too.

After trundling along all day, stopping randomly for hours, we eventually reached the border after dark. And it was dark in every way, as the Aymara had blacked it out to continue their smuggling. We all had to pile out at Charaña, a completely lawless border town, and sit on the freezing platform for over five hours, in a howling wind and pitch dark, until the Chilean train appeared. After it had dispensed its passengers, who were heading for La Paz, we had the usual frantic rush for seats, warding off pickpockets and bag snatchers. Luckily Gordon came into his own, and managed to grab seats while I followed slowly in the rear, dragging the luggage. The engine kept flashing its powerful headlamps onto the platform, then blacking out and hooting furiously. It was impossible to see anything.

Once on board, we sat in a siding for a monotonously long time, while our passports were stamped, and luggage gone through by good-looking Chilean customs men in heavy, long coats. I was stunned with cold, but by 3.30 in the morning we were on our way. Rattling along. Chile at last.

REUNITED WITH FRIENDS, AND CHANCE ENCOUNTERS IN CHILE

The First Time Ever I Saw Your Face

The antique British train rattled through the night, dawn waking us, after an hour's fitful doze, to the sight of the Atacama Desert. I could see the front of the train snaking ahead through dramatic mountains toned with the subtle colours of a parched land. Back again amongst sculptural, austere sand dunes rising far into the distance. As the heat grew stronger, I stripped off my poncho, then layers of jerseys, chewing the last few toffees, already sticky in my bag, their sugar giving a much-needed lift. Soon it was hot and, desperate for cool air, impossible to believe only a few hours earlier we had been cold to the bone. Through the open windows, burning wind blew as if from a hairdryer on full throttle, and as we slid on, all of a sudden, unexpectedly amongst hazy, fertile green valleys, we began to make out the dark line of the Pacific Ocean separating land from sky.

After twenty-four hours on the train, we clattered into Arica.

Letter

Arica's a sweet little port, the most northern in Chile. Exuberant and charming, it's sophisticated compared with places I've seen in other countries. A characteristic that's hit me, even on the train as we crossed the border, is the European-ness of the people. Men here are tall and good-looking; women, slim and elegant. They say when a foreigner arrives in Chile, his neck aches for the first three

days he's so busy gazing at the girls. And jeans are IN. Everyone
seems to be wearing them. Such a contrast to the last few months.

The little town was filled with cafés and enticing small shops, trees
lined the streets, thronged with gregarious locals. Down at the
harbour, bald-headed boys were diving for fish as boats came in on
a sparkling sea. I encountered a Bolivian touting for business, who
hustled me round the back of a shed, and changed my dollars into
escudos, before I succumbed to a dreamless sleep in a narrow bed
for $1 a night above a tiny flower shop.

The following day, having tried many times without success to
speak to Maria Luisa, my beloved friend, and desperately hoping
she was still in Santiago, we climbed on to the Pull-Bus Norte for the
thirty-three-hour journey south. It was she I had travelled so far to
see again after our flat-sharing in Madrid, but much had happened
politically since then: Chile had been in turmoil, and many people's
lives turned upside down. I left messages with a man who answered
the telephone, dubious that they would reach their destination. He
seemed not to understand what I was saying.

The bus was Super-Deluxe, with a television and airline loo. The
road was smooth, so I was able to doze between bouts of reading
Aku-Aku, about Easter island, far west off Chile's coast. As we sped
alongside the ocean, through the desert, where nitrate and copper
mines proliferated, we were frequently stopped for anti-fruit-fly
checks, *aduanas* polite and apologetic as they searched us all for
fruit that might harbour this invasive pest.

Antofagasta loomed large and industrial, with Pacific waves
thundering in when we stopped for food, and as day rolled into
night, the bus fell silent as passengers settled themselves for sleep.

Around midnight we were stopped for yet another *mosca de fruta* search, passengers grumbling as they were disturbed, having to stand up and open bags overhead and under seats, but the chattering soon ceased, and a cacophony of snores enveloped me.

We woke to find ourselves in La Serena, where we stopped for a much-needed breakfast of universal *revueltos* (scrambled eggs) and coffee. It looked an attractive colonial town, with wooden balconies and omnipresent tree-lined cobbled streets. We stretched arms and legs, bending and twisting until the driver hit the horn, and once again our journey continued relentlessly, south, until the desert was left behind and we entered scenery like the Wild West: cacti, scrub and ichu grass, whose pale feathery fronds shimmered as they blew in the breeze like a sea of blonde hair. Turning inland away from the Pacific, we climbed high into the foothills of the Andes, winding up before meandering down. Land looked fertile, a few farms appeared, followed by fruit trees, maize and rivers.

Meanwhile the loo on the bus smelled awful. All the windows were open but still it was disgustingly hard to take. My knees ached from being bent in the same position, not just for hours, but for days, and as Santiago finally came into view, I let out a whoop of excitement, noisily echoed by everyone else on board.

And there were my beloved friends, waiting while the beast of a bus slid into its space, and an assortment of dirty travellers hobbled down the steps. I'd made it – six months on the road to get here, and oblivious as to much that had gone on politically in the recent past.

I had heard tales from travellers heading north that the democratically elected Marxist, President Allende, had been deposed in a coup the previous year, led by General Pinochet, commander in chief of the Chilean army. (After years of speculation that Allende had been assassinated, his body was exhumed, and it was confirmed from gunshot wounds that he had killed himself.) All was far from well. A curfew was still in place; anyone caught breaking it was shot on sight, tanks roamed the streets, gunfire at night, thousands of people disappeared. It was clear that much depended on which side of the political fence you pinned your banner.

I had no idea what to expect, and imagined a downbeat reunion. But Maria Luisa and her family appeared full of the joys of a perfect autumn, as we fell into each other's arms. I was so in need of that hug. The sun shone with potent strength, throwing light through the tree-lined streets of an exclusive suburb where they lived, and unobstructed views lengthened east to the majestic snow-covered Andes.

Gordon was billeted with Maria Luisa's sister and her husband; the relief was intense. I hadn't realised how much my patience had been challenged by the annoying spume of inane questions, of slow, childlike misunderstandings. I hadn't recognised how much this kind, well-meaning, slow-witted Englishman had exasperated me. But he had been crucial for the physical travelling in so many ways, seizing seats, heaving bags and giving others much to laugh at. Now I was free to speak Spanish all the time, to share Maria Luisa's comfortable bedroom, and talk through the nights, catching up, reminiscing, wondering what the future held for us both.

She had returned to study at the recently reopened university, where many tutors and students had vanished. Rumours of torture and murder were in everyone's minds, along with a determination, for those who could, to step ahead of the horrors.

I joined the family on a visit to their vineyards, south of Santiago in the wine-growing region. Dozens of workers formed a scene out of a movie, as they picked grapes that would create the red wine for which the place was famous. Harvesters were bent over their work, chatting quietly, knotted scarves on their heads, and all stood up grinning as we approached. We stayed in their old family farmhouse, cracked occasionally by earthquakes, filled with brass bedsteads, religious paintings, cool flagstones over which bustled a team of stout, smiling maids. Stables were filled with horses ridden cowboy style, and Labradors roamed around wagging their tails. It was both foreign and yet familiar. Those Labradors could have been in any English garden; the women had their hair 'done' like my mother's. I could barely believe I was at the bottom of the world and not in a European country closer to home.

We visited their friends for lunch, another vineyard owner: Señor Zegers was a once-famous polo player, with a string of fifty polo ponies in the fields. Charming and gentle, he discussed Chilean politics with me in Spanish so fast I only understood one word in three. Everyone here seemed to cut off the ends of words, and my concentration was severely tested and found profoundly inadequate. He was frustrated that few people abroad, in his view, understood what was really going on, how the present military junta was simply branded as fascist. They had saved Chile from financial oblivion and a takeover by Russia. Did I realise there were twenty Russian warships waiting off the southern coast of Chile before the coup which deposed Allende? I had heard so many stories from different perspectives, it was hard then to make any judgement for myself.

Letter

There were about twenty-five of us, and we could almost have been in England with Labradors sniffing about, photographs on side tables of our host with Prince Philip or Lord Cowdray. He took us for a long, slow walk to watch cows being milked by hand. Blackberries, streams, weeping willows and always the delicious scent of eucalyptus trees. We returned to the house in time for an enormous tea – something the Chileans hold precious, and sat round a huge table with spotless white cloth, tucking into sandwiches, cakes, biscuits and, best of all, coffee rather than tea.

Politics aside (I was then naively unaware of Pinochet's secret police and the vast number of people hunting for disappeared members of their families), people I met were openly kind and friendly, a rarity that allowed me to feel happy and included, even if I didn't understand every word they said.

Back in Santiago we watched polo matches from lawns surrounded by splendid, ancient trees, leaves beginning to turn from deep green to their autumnal display, always the Andes sparkling behind. Bright-eyed, good-looking men were watched by model-perfect girls with dark hair and manicured nails. I was attracted to all of them, conscious my travel-worn clothes looked shabby beside such glamour, although no one seemed to care.

The ritual of teatime existed in the city too. No sooner had we finished a three-course lunch, with pisco sours, fresh fish and bowls of fruit, than plates of scones, cake and dulce de leche would arrive a couple of hours later and everyone tucked in again. Strong black coffee was always served in polished silver pots, creating a distorting canvas for those of us sitting around the bulbous convex shapes.

Maria Luisa's father, Jorge, a short, dapper man who treated me as another daughter, gave me a lift into the centre of town, the Plaza de Armas, where I changed my Green Beans, dollars borrowed from Gordon, on the black market at a great rate. Euphoria, as I worked out that maybe I could stretch my travels a little longer.

The city lacked charm: overbearing, gaunt grey buildings were pockmarked with bullet holes, and heaps of rubble lay around from tank guns fired at close range. Men and women huddled in small groups, as I hunted along streets for an office that could sell me a ticket for passage by cargo boat, from Punta Arenas in the far south of Patagonia back up the Chilean coast. It took a long while to find the Empremar office, and even longer to find a bus back home. None of them would stop, as desperate people ran into the roads trying to cling on to their dilapidated sides. If the drivers were held up at traffic lights, even though engines were revving to sprint ahead as quickly as possible, there was a surge from the hordes to clamber on. When eventually I squeezed into a heavily overcrowded bus, I was pressed against a man who rubbed his groin into me, fingers everywhere. I couldn't move, it was vile, and then so difficult to extract myself that I had to plead with everyone around to let me get off at the right place. Not a great morning, but mission accomplished; I had reserved a cabin on the boat.

Gordon was invited for dinner, and I watched in horror as he sat himself next to my host, Señora Vergara, waved his knife and fork around in the air, and spoke to her loudly and slowly as if she was half-witted. I felt in some way responsible for him, and cringed at his manners, although thanks to the curfew he had to leave, allowing Maria Luisa and me to continue our night-time chatter, putting our worlds to rights. Who would we marry, where would we live, what had fate got in store?

Conversations were sprinkled with a new-found language. I loved the words Chileans used, as different from the Spanish of Spain as American is from English. *Salvaje* (savage) meant wonderful, *pololo* a boyfriend. Who wouldn't crave one?

I had an introduction to the British ambassador and his wife, so found my way to the imposing embassy to leave them a note, and hoped to catch up on news. But there were no old copies of any newspapers, so I forced myself onto a bus to look round churches and museums. Inside the Colonial Museum a handsome golden pheasant strutted around the galleries, little claws scuffling on the old, worn stone, while dusty glass cases proffered no more than rusty locks and keys.

Another friend from the Madrid days, Milo Barbarani, an Italian diplomat now based in Chile, took me for lunch. '*Cara* Sara.' He beamed as we hugged and relived the previous few years. The tiny restaurant had no name, it was part of a family house, with scrumptious seafood, where we gorged on raw mussels with lemon, *erizos*, scallops, salads and gallons of white wine. Those moments scrawled into my memories, and I felt unbelievably lucky to have a life of such variety.

Out of the blue, a card had arrived from John and Monica Barnett, coming to Chile from Lima on a fishing trip, inviting Gordon and me to dinner in Santiago. It was Gordon's last night and seemed a perfect way to wrap up his travels and send him on his way. We arrived, breathless, at the restaurant in the dark, having run much of the way unable to find a bus, and found a party of eighteen expats in full swing. The touristy place was packed, a stage at one end, musicians playing, and folk dancers who swirled around, wearing whatever was deemed a national costume. We had a genuinely warm reunion with our wonderful Lima hosts, all irritations forgotten. They were real friends.

As I regaled Monica of my planned route into southern Chile, she told me that her cousin was travelling around Patagonia, and soon on his way north to stay with them in Peru. 'Look out for him. He's called Bruce.' Before we had finished eating, we were interrupted by dancers trying to haul us onto the stage, and as the spotlight swirled overhead, I shrank, but too late, was dragged off to make a fool of myself. It was funny, we all laughed, not such a terrible ordeal, and as the hour of curfew loomed, everyone stood up to kiss cheeks goodbye, to make their way out and home before the tanks rumbled in.

Letter

I spent several days pottering around the centre of Santiago, getting to know it, and working out my trip south. If you look at a map of Chile, you'll see what an extraordinary shape it is. From desert in the north to icebergs and glaciers in the south. We could be on a different planet down here. There's a saying that when God made the world, he tossed all the leftovers over the Andes and thus formed Chile.

I almost missed lunch with the Secondes, the British ambassador and his wife, as I couldn't find a bus to the embassy, and by the time I got there he had gone, but left a chauffeur-driven Land Rover to take me to the residence, which is huge. As we drank Pimm's on the verandah, I was introduced to a smartly suited Brazilian minister and his funny little daughter. Uniformed staff ran around and fed us *tortolas*, tiny wild doves that the ambassador had shot, fresh raspberries and cream. I gathered he's having a tough time with Harold Wilson being so anti the junta in Chile, but they love actually living here.

Meanwhile Maria Luisa's classes were being cancelled, and most days she returned from an empty university. Shots rang out during the night and the comfort of a life I'd landed in felt surreal.

I hugged Gordon goodbye, suddenly apprehensive of being back on my own again, and sad in a way to be losing my annoying buddy, but knowing it was time to move on. There were no direct roads south, no buses, no trains, so, unable to find any other route, I threw my Green Beans to the wind and flew down to Punta Arenas in an old military prop plane, sitting at the back, unable to see much out of a cracked, steamed-up window. The steward chatted most of the way, both of us avoiding anything political, until we landed with a thud at the bottom of the world. A man in military uniform checked visas and passports, convinced that one of my photographs was of my mother, but he let me through, and I caught a bus in the cold silver-grey light along the shore of the Strait of Magellan into Punta Arenas. The air was raw.

My bible for the entire trip was the *1974 South American Handbook*. The hardback book contained 944 pages with details of the whole continent, full of history, useful tips, banking hours, advertisements for shipping lines and roughly sketched maps. I couldn't have moved without it. It told me that Punta Arenas had a British Club: 'Not what it used to be but reasonable, drinks and billiards good. It resembles a stage set from a Victorian melodrama'. The British vice-consul's office was at the same address, and I went to find him. Denley King was a charming Scotsman of eighty-four, who had lived in these parts all his life, and yet had an accent you could cut with a *sgian-dubh*, as if he'd left Glasgow a few days earlier. He spoke of the large British settlement down here, how limited communication was, few roads, no public transport, and that I really couldn't hope to travel to any of the places I wanted to visit. He could see I was disappointed, so took me into the Club where he gave me a strong gin and tonic, and I settled down to read faded, torn copies of British newspapers.

The centre of Punta Arenas had some handsome buildings where I found small cafés serving delicious empanadas, my staple diet all over Latin America. They were pastries filled with sweet or savoury ingredients, baked or fried, available almost everywhere, and I must have eaten many kilos of them in each country; stuffed with guinea pig in Ecuador, with black beans and chicken in Peru, or fish when near lakes or the ocean. Now at the bottom of the world, I also found 'Apple Kuchen with Cream' trumpeted – a sign of the large German settlements in Patagonia, tucked away, untroubled by the rest of the globe.

Having slept for hours under heavy blankets in a neat hostel and thwarted by the lack of any transport heading to the mountains, I started walking to the port, seabirds swooping over the deeply unfriendly sea. I had every layer of clothing I could fit on, and still the wind bit into me, tearing at whatever fragment of flesh it could find. A truck stopped to give me a lift to the Marika ferry, where I boarded the old tub to cross the Strait of Magellan to the largest island in the archipelago of Tierra del Fuego. The crossing was bumpy, and as I sat on the bridge deck in the sun, sheltering from the gale, I had to hold tight to the bench to stop being thrown around. After two and a half hours we found calmer waters, as the ferry steamed through the channel to the landing pier, where I ran out into the biting cold, touched the water, touched the ground, pocketed some stones and jumped straight back on board.

Journal

Tierra del Fuego looked beautiful in a dour way, with deep yellow rolling hills, and hundreds of birds flying in formation. It has the largest sheep station in the world. Now I've touched the most southerly point on my journey I feel I'm starting towards home. Difficult word to use. Sometimes I feel lonely within myself.

I had bought a ticket for the cargo boat that was to take a number of passengers up the treacherous channels of southwest Chile. Other than occasional weather-dependent flights, it was the only route north. Waiting for its departure, days passed with walks into the scrubby hills, divulging views to snow-covered mountains gleaming in the distance. I wrote letters home, and of thanks, on hideous cards given by Monica, to some of the many people who had unconditionally welcomed me into their lives. On my frequent outings to the post office, I watched other travellers, several over from the Falkland Islands, congregating to find a passage on the boat. They lived isolated lives. From out of my bedroom window the Strait of Magellan radiated the most brilliant of blues, with Tierra del Fuego translucent and deceptively close. The sky was piercing sapphire and the cold profound. I promised myself that I would return. (I did!)

Finally the moment arrived; a raw wind whipped through the crowd of people waiting on the quay. Already the sun had sunk below the wild strait and a dusky half-light threw shadows amongst the locals as they ushered their animals up the ramp and onto the ancient cargo boat. A full moon rose over the hills.

I watched the scene, mesmerised and cold to my bones. A handful of men stood around waiting to board. They were clearly not local, wearing battered tweeds, holding ancient leather suitcases, and although not obviously travelling together, they had the homogenous look of foreigners in this part of Patagonia.

A clear, precise English voice behind me asked no one and everyone, 'Do you think we can eat on board?' Surprised, I turned to see a tall blonde man in a thick black sweater, his penetrating blue eyes shining despite the dark. He smiled as he extracted himself out of his heavy backpack, put out his hand and said, 'Hello, I'm Bruce Chatwin.'

We were all joining this old tub of a boat which would deliver food to lighthouses and remote villages up the treacherous fjords, before reaching the island of Chiloé, and thence to Puerto Montt, where a road could take us further. We chatted, as most travellers finding a fellow compatriot do. Bruce had spent six months in Patagonia researching stories for a book he hoped to publish. I had spent over six months travelling down to Chile through Central and South America, arriving in countries with tanks in their streets, curfews and strikes. These were unsettled times, and Bruce had been out of touch with the rest of the world. He was heading north to Peru to join his wife Elizabeth, and to stay with a cousin in Lima. 'It must be Monica,' I exclaimed, incredulous that we should actually meet.

'I've been following her father's footsteps,' he laughed. 'He sent a piece of giant sloth skin from a cave here in Patagonia to my grandmother, and it's haunted me since I was a child.'

He sounded like a *Boy's Own* explorer, and I grinned in tentative anticipation of being regaled with romantic adventure stories.

'Let's share a table in the dining saloon,' he suggested as we both gratefully fell into a surprised bond of camaraderie and tales of mutual friends, watching over the side as a tug pulled us away from Punta Arenas, lights twinkling, and edged us into the strait.

Our cabins were wonderful. A small plaque informed me that the highly polished wood was English walnut, edged in shining brass. I even had an old-fashioned chest of drawers, a locker and a desk. I had paid $20 to go first class, everything included, in the hope I would be less prone to feeling seasick. This meant I ate in the dining room amongst the captain and officers, each table with its own steward. Food was simple and mountainous, enhanced by delicious bread freshly baked each day in the galley below. Second class looked rough, and in the bowels of the boat third was a malodorous nightmare of sick, smoke, babies and urine.

The *Navarino* was British built, in Poole in 1920, and had plied her trade along the coasts of Vietnam before crossing the world to Chile where she stoically weathered appalling blizzards, fearsome seas and treacherous rocks to ply this route. Her captain and crew were Chileans who went about their tough work with cigarettes hanging out of their mouths, gnarled hands pulling on ropes, checking hatches, and rolling with the sudden vehemence of enormous waves which battered the sides and flooded the decks.

Bruce spent his days shut in his cabin writing. I spent mine outside, chatting with the red-helmeted crew, watching spectacular grey whales spouting close to the boat, scrutinising desolate islands, terrifying jagged rocks and hulks of wrecks standing upright in the water, now reduced to skeletons. The poet Byron's great-grandfather had been shipwrecked off one of these godforsaken islands when his ship, the *Wager*, was hurled onto rocks. He managed eventually to escape, but most of his crew were not so lucky.

Journal

Staggered round the deck in a colossal swell with waves crashing. Could see land very clearly on both sides of the channel, towering, gaunt grey rocks lined with waterfalls and patches of snow – spray blown everywhere from the force of icy-cold wind howling. Lots of large gulls. Passed close to the vast wreck of SS *Santa Leonor*, an American ship which sank on rocks only seven years ago due to the American merchant navy using right and left for directions, instead of the globally recognised port and starboard. Its huge, bullet-riddled hulk, having been used for target practice by the Chilean navy, stuck straight up out of the water, eerie and mysterious.

Four-course lunch with Bruce Chatwin presiding. He's got Monica's habit of not listening unless he's really interested. A funny accent that's just too much, and yet he's compulsively likeable. Vital, strange and fascinating.

Blown around the deck, having fought to stagger round one corner, I was then jet propelled round the next and almost hurtled into the sea, eventually making it onto the bridge, and chatted with the charming captain. More polished brass and the radar working full-time. He too told me that just before Allende was deposed there were twenty Russian warships down near Punta Arenas, waiting.

Back to writing in our funny little lounge, played duets on the honky-tonk piano with an Englishman from Newcastle who's mad about steam engines, and who concocted a communal pisco sour for everyone in there. Bruce tore in and demanded one too, then lost his temper over stories of large companies buying farms in England, and looked just like Trotsky, white and shaking, before he swirled off, lurching around, to dinner.

Journal

Bitterly cold, a dirty sky, but clearer, so saw countless islands, fjords and channels. Blue ice and snow on the mountains, land tantalisingly close. Bruce, Monica in trousers, raced around the decks in an orange anorak being terribly serious, talking full pelt at everyone.

The captain blasted our horn as we anchored just off Puerto Edén, a tiny, forlorn hamlet. Greeted by hordes of wretched-looking, scrawny men in waterlogged canoes filled with mussels, dried, fresh and salted. Sealskin boats and reed baskets. They climbed up the sides of the ship using portholes as footholds, swarmed on board to sell their wares, a rather wonderful sight like bees around the honeypot. Then when we hooted again, they raced off and rowed ashore as fast as they could. Numbingly cold and desolate, it must be hard to thrive there.

Death was all around us as we lurched on through the storms and into the Golfo de Penas. We lost some of our cargo in the wild of one night, and were hove to for what seemed like days, unable to go backwards or forwards, just hoping we could hold on until the waves crashing over us subsided. I had never been in such terrifying seas but felt remarkably calm, knowing there was nothing I could do, except cling on.

Bruce and I managed somehow to meet for lunch and for dinner each day, sliding along passages to regale the other of hours spent. He told me stories of his time in Patagonia finding eccentric people to write about, of his time as a young director at Sotheby's (he was now thirty-four), of his ultimate boredom there, and his need to explore. He spoke of his friendship with my grandfather, Henry Denham, although I'd never heard his name mentioned, and with my cousin Alex Moulton, creator of the famous small-wheel bicycle, a brilliant engineer and designer who had first put suspension into the Mini car, into coaches and then into powerboats. When I reached England and asked Alex about their friendship, he waved it aside, not keen to have family know too much about his private life. Bruce told me about his wife Elizabeth, an American heiress who also enjoyed travelling, but in slightly greater comfort; she and Penelope Chetwode, poet John Betjeman's wife, regularly travelled in India together. He never stopped talking. He was magnetic and amusing. He was a snob who loved name-dropping. He was inspiring with his energy and enthusiasm, irritating in his narcissism. He had asked early on that I should never disturb him while he was writing, then was furious with me for not alerting him to the sights which surrounded the ship. During dinner he stood up and stamped his feet, trembling with rage that I hadn't told him there were whales spouting close by, nor called him to see the occasional sight of Indigenous people, wearing roughly devised sealskin, battling their canoes against the sea in a bid to survive another day. He wanted stories for his book.

Letter

Gradually we left the glaciers, penguins and rocky islands behind, and could see a few boxy houses dotted around as land became greener. We stopped at a miniscule fishing village to give them their month's supply of food, and in return they gave us smoked mussels and sold little baskets and model sealskin boats. I can't think how they survive in such wild weather for generations, within their small family units. Extraordinary seeing so many ghost ships, like monumental sentries lining our route, wrecked as recently as two years ago. They stand upright, rusted bows sinister as the sea hurls itself against them. Most of the islands are identified after British naval expeditions, and explorers wrecked centuries ago, who clung to life on one of these barren islands, including Monica's father, Charles Milward, wrecked while sailing out from Scotland. There is Isla James, Victoria, Fitz Roy, Simpson, Byron, Wager and Johnson to name a fraction of them. Remarkable how many brave and adventurous Brits have left their names in Patagonia.

I met the other passengers when they surfaced from the bowels of the boat for fresh air: local farmers with their goats and chickens penned up below; a few women in long thick skirts, scarves round their black hair; silent children hanging at their backs. The tweedy men came from South Georgia. They were monosyllabic and friendly, heading out for a better life somewhere else in the world. A pasty-faced man travelling with a dreadful Canadian couple and their screaming brat, who had made their fortune changing money on the black market, came from the Falkland Islands. There was a former farmer from Maryland with flaming-red beard and little round specs, a cinema manager from Chicago who I christened Andy Capp as he always wore a flat cap, tie and brown suit, whatever the weather. And an irritating man from who knew where, with dyed blonde hair, whom I named the Great Gatsby and tried to avoid. He was huge, and his voice carried everywhere, inside and out. We were a disparate bunch, and it was interesting chatting to them.

Every evening the travelling lingerie salesman, finally heading for home in an ill-fitting suit, emerged from below decks and played simple tunes on a battered piano in the dining room. The ship swayed, pitched and rolled before slamming down into incomprehensible depths. Passengers clutched at walls to make their way back to their bunks.

Letter

For some reason I felt terrifically well – and hungry. Bruce and I managed to get to the dining room, where waiters had already tucked into their supper and were amazed to see us. Needless to say it was only the mad English who managed to make it that night, but to our amused dismay, the waiter slithered towards us with a plate of pig's trotters – a great fatty mass in a watery gravy. It was enough to make anybody feel ill just looking at it, let alone having it almost flung into your lap every time the boat lurched up and down. As a result we've sworn to have a pig's trotter reunion to commemorate being tossed around in the Golfo de Penas, understandably known as one of the roughest seas in the world.

Bruce and I talked incessantly, laughing, fearful, filled with the joyous sense of an adventure way out of our hands.

I have never in my life been in such rough sea, and I can't understand how the boat plunged through those monumental waves which kept crashing way over the bridge decks, sweeping everything not screwed down over the side. One moment we did a complete circle, 360 degrees, and then were hove to for twenty-four hours, at a standstill, unable to move forwards.

It was frightening, and almost impossible to stand up for more than a second without being flung about. Like going up and down in an out-of-control lift. No one can have slept a wink during the nights, too busy clinging to our bunks to avoid being thrown out.

One morning the sea had calmed, and by lunchtime we were back inside the channels in comparatively sheltered water. The poor second- and third-class passengers had had a grim time down below, and few of them managed to stagger up on deck to gulp down some desperately needed fresh air. I sat on deck in the hazy sun, something that hadn't appeared since we sailed, watching storm petrels and white albatrosses flying past, waiting for the sound of a xylophone rattling, the ship's equivalent of a gong announcing the next meal.

Journal

Castro on Chiloé Island came into view as I rubbed my eyes open and pressed against the salt-encrusted porthole. A small straggle of gaily coloured wooden houses climbed up the hillside, a large red church dominating the top. Scenery had completely changed overnight, and patchwork-quilt islands spread out on a calm lake-like sea. Rolling hills, tiny fields, thick hedges, poplar trees. Exquisite and exciting.

Many of the passengers left, stumbling down the gangplank, crumpled and wobbly. It would be a while until they found their land legs again. Bruce also left, having persuaded me to keep his heavy red duffel bag of books and take them to the ship's office in Puerto Montt. He strode away without a backward glance, trailing some sense of the legend and enigma he was to become. His book, *In Patagonia*, would take the literary world by storm, and create a whole new genre of writing.

I wandered along the quay, watching horses and carts loaded with cargo from our hold, including hundreds of dark green empty wine flagons in caskets of woven willow. My legs felt unstable, my stomach queasy, until the siren boomed its familiar signal, and remaining passengers climbed up the ramp for the final time. I wished the journey could continue for longer, but all too soon we had left the peaceful island behind, and were heading too fast towards Puerto Montt, and the end, or the beginning, of the road. I was still evading the Great Gatsby as he thundered around the decks in his outsize dark glasses, tweed jacket and tie flapping, signs of a blonde moustache emerging. As he hollered my name, I slipped furtively into the dining room to have one final tea of hot fresh bread, apricot jam with thick butter, served by Antonio, who hugged me goodbye: 'Adios, Miss Café.'

In the setting sun, Puerto Montt's harbour was small and narrow, giving *Navarino* and the captain a hard time manoeuvring alongside. Carlos, one of the crew, a storyteller full of fun with whom I'd had long conversations, helped me drag Bruce's heavy bag to the little hut which served as ticket office for the ship, where they refused to take it in until the captain appeared, and suddenly it was all over, and I was back on the mainland, once more having to find my way.

Still lurching around, I attempted to walk out my sea legs under the carved wooden balconies of Bavarian-style wooden houses. They filled the sides of narrow streets like chalets, interspersed with gaily lit shop signs spelling out their German names.

Letter

There's a large German population in southern Chile from the industrial slump in Europe in the 1940s, when they came over, along with refugees from both sides in the war. As a result there are loads of delicious cheese and charcuterie shops, hot chocolate cafés with scrumptious homemade cakes, and clean, efficiently run little hotels. Beside the sprawling fish market, nets and paraphernalia from local boats lie drying on tin roofs.

Small buses transported me into the soft countryside, whose rolling fields were ploughed by oxen trawling wooden carts. Wildflowers, harvest, deep lakes, large Germanic houses of slatted wood and neat, flower-filled gardens. I walked miles gorging on plump, juicy blackberries, purple juice staining my fingers, while beyond the lakes posed perfect snow-capped volcanos. No longer having Gordon at my side, I was happy to be alone, pondering, dreaming and wondering. I met more people again, sat and talked to strangers, was helped with my case. Definitely better without the man.

One evening, beside a log fire while I wrote letters, the television showed an ancient British film, *North West Frontier*, with Kenneth More, Wilfrid Hyde-White and Lauren Bacall on a train in India. Funny with Spanish subtitles, it had me giggling at the ultra Britishness of the language, and the incongruity of having this in front of me while I was in such a remote corner of the world.

Each night along with writing my journal, I counted all my remaining money, working out how much longer I could continue travelling. I still had the return air ticket from Rio de Janeiro stashed in the bottom of my case, but the Green Beans were going fast.

Journal

Life is 'fascinating' – a word Bruce C used incessantly, and accused me of too. Kept bumping into the awful Gatsby, and Falklander, the silent Falkland Islander in his mountaineering kit, with the same battered hat on top of his spiky face. Where are they going?

As the sun rose, catching dew on the grass, I pulled my case to the bus that would take me towards the lake crossing from Chile into Argentina, and saw to my horror the dreaded American couple, Bob and Cathy, and their squawking brat. Also waiting were the Gatsby and Falkbender. Not such a big world after all. The journey took all day, in vintage buses across several small islands, and on small vessels across fathomless turquoise lakes that drifted into rivers where salmon plopped and jumped, and waterfalls spilled down steep, forested mountainsides. A straggle of passengers, we climbed on and off our different modes of transport, while colours of autumn charged leaves of ancient trees with umbers and oranges, beginning to turn in the cooler air. I picked ever-present enormous blackberries as we walked between buses and boats, keeping the Americans well out of earshot, watching bright butterflies landing delicately on ferns and grasses. A small jetty spread out into a lake where Argentine customs checked everything I possessed, including my illegible journal; a remote and romantic border crossing. Chugging across translucent green water as the sun dipped, I searched out the warmth of a seat below deck, and found myself wedged between Gatsby and an Argentinian woman with wild hair, and make-up deep enough to bury treasure, who wouldn't draw breath. On and on she prattled as I attempted to read my book. I wanted to throttle her. Gatsby with his deep voice and interminable questions was no better, while Falkbender sat on his other side in agitated silence.

Letter

I can't tell you how beautiful the scenery is, hard to absorb such glorious surroundings. Each lake has mountains iced with snow in the background, ringed by forested volcanos and undulating hills. It was a boiling day with not a cloud in the sky when we reached Lago Todos los Santos, wildflowers and magnificent trees cascading down to the water's edge. It's a fisherman's paradise. On each lake men stand waist deep, watchful as herons, casting lines far out into the still water. Pa, you'd go mad.

Once across the lake, on an island, we squashed into a trailer, pulled by an antique tractor, and had a disgusting lunch at vast expense in a German-run hotel, before setting off again. A gravelled track snaked through a parkland of woods and swing bridges. At last we reached San Carlos de Bariloche, supposedly one of the prettiest little towns in Argentina. It's built entirely like a Bavarian village, has good skiing nearby, although now is not the season.

Isabel Perón, the widow of President Juan Perón, and now herself president of Argentina, was arriving to stay in the renowned hotel beside the lake where we left the little ferry. Banners and flags were out in force, bunting waving in the breeze. But the ski resort and local town of Bariloche beckoned, as I teamed up with a chic, neat French girl, travelling alone, sharing a room with her for an expensive $4, feasting on steak and wine, and wishing time would slow down. She looked incongruous in Gucci shoes, a Dior handbag and smart skirt, although perhaps it was I, in my battered jeans, frayed shirt, who looked out of place. The town was humming with tall, good-looking Argentinian men and women, and as I gazed about, Marie Lournes talked of her life. It transpired that she lived with her strict parents in Paris, who had an estate in the Loire, which she insisted I visit when we both returned to Europe. It sounded surreal and very far away.

After a few days exploring the mountainous country around Bariloche, I waved au revoir to Marie Lournes beside the lake glistening in early morning sun, and by a whisker caught a bus heading towards La Unión, on which an irritating man failed to enthuse the passengers to sing along with him. By midday, I was sitting on a log under slender Lombardy poplars, leaves vibrant yellow against an azure sky, eating a picnic of melted chocolate, having crossed the border back into Chile. I chatted to a couple from Hawaii who had also met Bruce Chatwin in Patagonia. Jack had sailed across oceans around the world and told stories in a hypnotic drawl. I thought he was terrific. He wasn't so sure about Bruce.

Letter

La Unión is a small town in picturesque farming country. I went into a little store, to ask how to find Lago Ranco, where a handsome woman buying newspapers heard me and said she'd help. Señora Le Loup turns out to be head of a local college, and took me to her office, where she telephoned bus and railway stations, efficiently gathering information about departures and costs. Her unattractive, overweight secretary, squeezed into Bariloche jeans, which are all the rage, lips slathered with vermilion lipstick, tossed my heavy case over her shoulder and took it, plus me, to a cheap, clean German hotel, where I share the only bathroom with the large family who own it. I've never seen so many toothbrushes parked around a basin.

I couldn't believe the warmth to a total stranger when the director invited me to dinner with her family; three daughters and a Belgian husband, who is weedy, and speaks so fast and so quietly I can't make out a word. She talked about Allende and how terrible his time in office was, how hard everyone is working now to unite Chile, how they've avoided communism, while we in Europe are heading towards it. Listening, as I chewed fresh bread spread with homemade rosehip jam, I watched, through the window, a full moon rising, lighting up the rural landscape. Seeing fields of cows, dew in the grass, and oak trees, it feels familiar, a sense of much that I subconsciously miss after so many months of heat and desert.

Chile, filled with anomalies.

Señor Le Loup, the Belgian husband, runs the only linen factory in Chile, and it was 'fascinating', as Bruce would say, seeing the process from raw flax to the woven material, watching the techniques of dyeing and weaving. I noticed all the machinery came from Belfast.

I see King Faisal's been assassinated by a mad nephew. Great shock and will presumably cause chaos.

Long bus journeys on unpaved roads delivered me to remote farms, more lakes in which fishermen caught shiny silver salmon and brought them to families where I stayed. Supper was always a simple feast of local produce with copious amounts of wine. By day, gauchos rode horses through the fields, wrapped in ponchos, feet in carved wooden stirrups, sheepskin-covered saddles, stopping to chat with friends along their way. And each day I walked for hours, alongside fast-flowing rivers, where startled geese and ducks flew up from reeds, the air thick with butterflies. I talked to farmers ploughing with oxen, to occasional policemen on huge horses, and to the old men who worked a tiny chain ferry across the water. It was a land of milk and honey, an Eden which outwardly bore no relation to the nightmares in Santiago, way up north.

Journal

Easter tomorrow. Staying a few days with a family above their shop in Llifén. Heard rain pattering on the tin roof all night, and felt snug in bed. But eventually struggled up, grabbed apples from the tree outside, and crackled off in my pacamac to Maihue Lake, fourteen kilometres there and fourteen back. Passed huge oxen pulling wooden carts with heavy yokes on their heads, little wooden shacks with chickens and barefooted children, gauchos cantered by. My feet aching in Señora Vergara's borrowed shoes. Eventually reached the lake, and sat on an upturned boat in a heap. Pretty with forested hills all around, wooden houses with smoke wafting up, horses and cattle grazing, waterfalls. Almost too perfect to be true. Black-necked swans gliding around, and geese pecking and hissing furiously. Reluctantly set off again and trudged all the way back, daydreaming of home, where will it be, how will I arrive, what will I do, and what will Ma and Pa do. Feet hurting miserably, but made it all the way, and tucked into a huge tea before an enormous dinner, where a group of fat fishermen stared at me, especially a revolting one in a red anorak. Through the window, swirling mists made me feel almost dizzy as clouds zoomed in on the mountains and an elderly blind man in a huge poncho, tapping his stick, tramped past.

Journal

Already it's Easter Day. So hard to believe.

Walked all morning, eating an entire bar of chocolate as an Easter present to myself, and returned to the family for a vast lunch; attempted again to avoid the stares of paunchy fishermen, especially one who looked like a walrus, and the wretched red anorak number. Chased by two huge pigs when I went down to the lake, so lay on my bed reading Scott Fitzgerald's *This Side of Paradise*; Amory Blaine reminds me of Sebastian Flyte in *Brideshead*, or even Mungo in *Mungo's Dream*. Having dreaded the bill for staying here all these days, it came to £5. Amazing value.

Days drifted by and time came to leave this paradise. So, once more, up before dawn, groping downstairs in the dark and out into the lane, where dawn was lazy, cockerels crowed and river birds bellowed. The same old red bus that had delivered me stopped to pick me up, so full I had to stand for several hours. Sheep shat on my case on the roof, chickens squawked just above my head and a man with two ducks pressed me from behind.

After five antique bus changes, the sweet village of Pucón finally came into view as the sun was setting. Yellowing poplars stood on the banks next to willows weeping over streams. Ice-capped volcano Villarrica stood spectacularly tall above the clouds as light faded.

Journal

Lay in sun looking at twinkling (horrid word), sparkling (better) blue water, condors cawing overhead, orange and yellow butterflies flitting about. I remember Bruce Chatwin saying the greatest thing about the English language is the verb, and a good author ought to make full use of them…

Seeing so many horses everywhere, I asked a local farmer if I could rent one for a day, and explore the countryside around. He eventually appeared with a lame carthorse, Thelwell-style, with an enormous saddle, and a tiny bay pony, its ears flat back. I clambered onto the carthorse, which could barely walk, switched to the bad-tempered pony, which refused to budge, despite a boy behind who hissed at it as uselessly as I kicked. No go.

And so again, I walked, dreaming of familiar home food – shepherd's pie, cauliflower cheese, treacle tart and cream – returning late as a sunset over the lake reflected pink light off snow-capped volcanos into the water.

Letter

Leaves have fallen off the trees. It's autumn here now, feeling slightly sad and cold.

Back with sweet Maria Luisa who is the nicest possible person and a real friend. Her parents are adorable, he calls me '*hijita*' – daughter – and is trying frantically to stop me from leaving, saying this is my house. When I tell anyone I don't want to go, they all say, 'Well, stay then.' It doesn't help.

Pepa, my other great friend from Madrid, is engaged to an architect from Spain, and Jaime arrived this week, much to her enormous family's amusement. Poor man has been subjected to endless 'meet the relations' parties. He's a funny little fellow, nervous, smart and painfully shy. He proposed over the telephone, and now they have just four weeks until the wedding, so a mad rush to get it all organised. I spent an afternoon with her looking at pictures of wedding dresses, then couldn't find a bus back to Maria Luisa, and got so cold waiting that I hitched a ride in a passing car.

Journal

Incredibly tough meat for dinner with all the Vergara family sitting round. I'm such a slow eater that I was left in silence, embarrassingly hacking away at whatever animal it had been, rocking the silver on the table.

I had meanwhile fallen for Stephen, an Englishman living in Chile, divorced and, at forty-two, old enough to be my father.

Journal

At a lunchtime assignation he arrived, looking devastating. Dark hair greying at the sides, tinted specs, long limbed with beautiful hands. He is the sweetest, gentlest man. Over pisco sours we talked about everything and anything; the world crises, all that's happened in the past month while I've been travelling. Kissinger's failed in the Middle East, Vietnam is on the verge of communism, and Saigon will fall soon. Portugal is in chaos. The world seems to be sinking. I find him disarming, and told him about Ma and Pa, my life in Spain. He asked why I wouldn't come and live in Chile. I blushed and probably didn't answer. The thought of him gives me butterflies, possibly because he's the first attractive man I've met in six months, but I must move on. I'm almost out of visa time and funds.

Day trips to the Pacific with ML and her brothers in a shared red car, whose door kept flying open as we switchbacked through the scrubby red-earthed mountains, and down to the fishing villages often swathed in mist, while huge phosphorescent green waves rolled in, white spume spraying far away. We explored the 'snob' (a Chilean expression) areas of thatched houses on wild beaches, and unspoilt Zapallar, a glorious bay with a sprinkling of large houses (apparently the centre of scandal and orgies), eucalyptus and pines down to the water.

We ate seafood I had never heard of, and as we walked the beach one day there was a violent earth tremor, a shocking shudder under our feet. Quick but dramatic. The epicentre was hundreds of miles away, but the sensation of helplessness and fear remained a long while.

I dreamed of Stephen, knowing it was hopeless, yet the attraction was so strong I couldn't wave it away. Annoyingly it gnawed into my stomach. The logic of a lost cause played no truck with my imagination. When I confided in Maria Luisa she smiled and told me every woman who met him found him irresistible.

Journal

Went to the shabby cinema downtown and watched a film in Italian with Spanish subtitles, *The Garden of the Finzi-Continis*. Slow and deep, filled with melancholy and eccentricity, it suggests that to fully appreciate life you have to metaphorically die at least once, and it's better to die young so that you have more time to recover.

Conversations with ML's parents of their time living in the States revealed that when the children were young, they wouldn't eat anything cooked by a Black person, as they had never seen one before. There were none living in Chile. They also told me Americans they met assumed most Chileans wore feathers in their hair and rings in their noses.

I chatted in the kitchen most mornings with the lovely Carmen, who lived with and worked for the family. While she made breakfast, as the others slept, she told me about her husband living with another woman, her children living with their grandparents. I bought her little presents, and wondered if this would be her life for evermore. We tiptoed around politics.

Journal

Sloshed through fallen leaves in parks to meet Stephen. Heightened awareness of everything around, the clarity of autumn light, anticipation. In San Agustin church, Christ's crown of thorns fell from his head during an earthquake, and is now painfully around his neck. It can't be moved. He has a fierce expression on his tortured, bloody face, and I ponder again why religion gets in the way of God.

Maria Luisa accompanied me to dinners with Stephen and his middle-aged friends from around the globe. They were friendly, mostly married and, in their forties, seemed old. Whenever I was in conversation with an American banker, or Brazilian writer, I could hear Stephen's voice somewhere near, saw him out of the corner of my eye, and wouldn't relax until he came to sit close, full of compliments and desire to keep me in Chile. I was so tempted. Then someone would remind us that the curfew hour was imminent, and we all grabbed coats, hugged goodbyes and left in a hurry. At night tanks were still rumbling the streets, patrols marching narrow lanes, shots rat-a-tatting. I was floating on the superficial surface of a historical drama, when thousands of people disappeared, lethally punished for their political beliefs. The new junta, under General Pinochet, brutally accepted zero opposition.

Journal

Long discussions with Stephen about the usual: Darwin's theory, Christianity, politics, how he suddenly needed a break from the dreary people he worked with in England. Now he's at a crossroads, intensely attractive and exciting. But I don't want to be snared by imagination. That old friend Mr Fate will play his hand.

And so, early morning a few days later saw me climbing into a bus bound for Mendoza in Argentina. There were no tears of farewell; I knew I would return. We all laughed and hugged in the dusky dawn of Santiago's terminal. I was grateful beyond words to know I had another family in beautiful Chile, who would never fail to welcome me into their lives. My motivation for travelling the length of South America had always been to reach this faraway ribbon of a country and see my cherished friends. I'd made it, collecting more memories and soulmates along the way.

LUXURY AND CHAOS IN ARGENTINA

You Don't Have To Say You Love Me

I sat on a seat near the front, only to be turned out by an overweight Peruvian in a silly hat too small for his bulbous head. Encouraged by other passengers shouting excitedly, I held my ground, until he physically dragged me off. So, seeing as he wasn't there, I settled down in the conductor's chair, next to the driver, where I soon boiled under a fierce sun blazing through the windscreen. But the astounding views, as if from an aeroplane, more than compensated for such hothouse discomfort as we snaked high into the Andes, driven round the bend, more than literally, by the Peruvian's imbecilic remarks as he noisily chewed grapes, sucking and blowing on them, spitting the pips out onto the floor. Then his wife was sick, missing me by inches. Followed by their granddaughter. The driver groaned. We continued upwards past Portillo, the main ski centre on this side of the world. Stationary chairlifts and the only hotel, like an enormous child's model, looked grey against glistening, snow-covered peaks, and the immense, silent lake behind it reflected a cloudless blue sky.

We exited Chile at the top of a pass, disappearing through a long, dusty tunnel, and emerged, blinking, on the Argentinian side of the mountains. Customs officers were smart and polite, quickly processing our passports so we could continue, and an old man flicked a feather duster over our filthy bags on the roof, holding out his hand for a tip. There was an issue with the Peruvians' passports, which held us up, and as soon as we were impatiently on our way, the wife was sick again. An entire busload, a mixture of Chileans, Ecuadorians, Bolivians and Argentines, let out a collective moan.

Journal

Thrilling drive, a little like the Bolivian Zongo Valley, with fabulous coloured barren hills, wild rock formations streaked with minerals, green rivers rolling down the steep multicoloured earth. As we descended into fertile valleys, magnificent yellow-gold poplars stood in rows, waving gently in the breeze, like watchmen to my lost dreams. Romantic, a little sad and totally lovely.

This was the famous cordillera, an unforgettable four-hour drive towards Mendoza, known around the world for its superb wine.

The attractive colonial town was surrounded by miles of vineyards on all sides, but I wasn't stopping, and at the terminal managed to get the last seat on an overnight long-distance bus to Buenos Aires, gratified that I'd beaten the Peruvians to the ticket office. Thus, relinquished of my grape-sucking, vomiting companions, I settled down for a twenty-four-hour journey across the pampas.

Letter

The pampas are different from my imagination. Flat, yes, but broken into fields with thick hedges, woods with enormous, elegant trees, and greenest green grass everywhere. The country is unimaginably fertile. We passed huge estancias, fifty to sixty thousand acres an average, with hundreds of sleek horses grazing, plus herds of fat cattle, too many to count. The land yields several crops a year without fertilisers. I'm told that each adult drinks an average of a hundred litres of wine a year (couple of pints a day). All is on a vast scale: large, low houses, hordes of colourful gauchos, cowboy hats, bandanas round their waists, galloping across the pampas, lassoing cattle or playing polo. A huge steak, salad and vino costs around 20p. Aeroplanes parked like cars skip from one estancia to another to cover the huge distances. The prosperity seems extraordinary after most of the other South American countries. They slaughter about forty thousand head of cattle a day for home consumption, so delicious beef costs less than a glass of mineral water. Leather too, as you can imagine, is abundant. Labourers wear Gucci-like shoes costing £3 a pair. Suitcases, gloves, belts, are handmade, cheap and fabulous, but sadly after seven months on the move, these are untouchable temptations.

Although the affluence and wealth is staggering, I'm always aware they live on a knife-edge within their chaotic political situation. If you have dollars your world is cheap. The house I'm now staying in, in a smart part of BA, rented by Pepa's Chilean sister and her family, which has a swimming pool and five bedrooms, costs £40 a month.

BA is the eighth largest city in the world. Everyone I'd met told me that I'd love it as it's so European, which made me think I wouldn't, as it's just what I wanted to get away from. But it really is exciting. The centre is beautifully laid out, with wide, tree-lined boulevards, Parisian-style buildings, museums, colonial churches and the best shopping streets I've seen anywhere. One hundred per cent better than London, with nothing as shabby as Oxford Street. There's even a Harrods. The city's full of bustle and noise, terrible traffic; it pulsates with life, good restaurants, nightclubs, which after the curfew in Chile feels liberating.

But as always, there is massive political trouble, and the same old story; no one knows what will happen. Kidnappings and killings are frequent, and, according to friends whose entire conversations hinge on a daily dose of horror stories, seem to be getting worse. Families retain permanent bodyguards, they're threatened, their children snatched, and they live in a constant state of tension and nerves. But still the good living goes on, and the millionaires increase. It's extraordinary.

To put you in the political picture, Juan Perón died last year, aged seventy-eight, having returned to Argentina from exile in 1973. He won the election, promising to fight for the workers, but was a ruthless president, savagely suppressing all opposition.

(He had been married to the famous Eva Perón, who died in 1952 aged thirty-three. Evita had become a famous, powerful, unofficial leader of Argentina, revered by impoverished workers, especially the women.)

Juan's third wife, Isabel, whom he appointed vice president, is a dancer, disliked and resented by many Argentinians. She inherited the presidency when he died in July last year, becoming the world's first woman president. She has no support or power base, which is why terrorism, lawlessness and political violence are rampant.

In March 1976 armed forces took power, removed Isabel Perón from office and set up a junta, which for seven years viciously manoeuvred against suspected dissidents, murdering up to thirty thousand opponents, and many innocent civilians.

There were, on the other hand, those relieved as law and order gradually returned.

I was there in May 1975. Isabel had signed a secret presidential decree three months earlier in February, ordering the army to illegally annihilate an insurgency of around a hundred people from the smallest province in Argentina, inspired by the ideals of Che Guevara. This caused widespread protests, savagery and violence around the country. It was confusing as a foreigner to know what on earth was going on. And as with all politics, my understanding depended on whom I spoke to.

Letter

It's a perfect climate here now, the heat and humidity of summer is over, and I'm back in my faithful old jeans amongst the glamorous locals. The latest vogue is to turn them up at the bottom, and they're all following this fad like lemmings.

The day after I arrived, I was whisked off by Carlos, an Argentinian friend I knew in Madrid, to an area called Tigre, and on to the delta of the Paraná, a maze of channels and islands in the vast mouth of the Rio de la Plata, or River Plate. These areas cover hundreds of miles filled with tiny islands, home to small farms, restaurants or smart weekend houses. Thick vegetation hangs over narrow canals, which broaden out into wide channels, and then into the huge river itself.

A large speedboat, belonging to Chilean Roberto, reflected us all in its gleaming chrome, and as we waterskied, their friends raced alongside waving and laughing. Roberto was much too pleased with himself, and Carlos was nice but nervy. The Argentinians are open and friendly, although I don't find these famous tall dark men handsome. They're too much – give them a smile and they think you're at least engaged to them.

Tigre is another world, something out of a Bond movie. Cavernous warehouses are filled to the roof with speedboats, while gin palaces, yachts and powerboats appear around every corner of the river. Tying up to leap ashore for lunch on an island reminded me of a rural version of Venice; all life on the water. Fruit shops sail past, barges filled with wine chug by. When the heavens opened, we raced for home, queuing up amongst other speedboats, where a kind of pickup machine lifts them out of the water and delicately positions them onto a rack, and then into their special parking slot.

I spent most of the week sightseeing: the famous pink presidential Casa Rosada, where Eva Perón had made emotional speeches to crowds of thousands; churches; galleries; and Recoleta Cemetery, packed tight with huge mausoleums boasting altars and polished brass, like a mass of Wendy houses. Evelyn Waugh breezed into my mind. I gazed into shop windows like a child at Christmas; the first truly sophisticated ones I've seen since Mexico, and a thousand times better than those. Beautifully cut clothes, leather to tempt a vegetarian, everything beautifully displayed, and apparently thriving, although all the money changers are closed as the dollar has risen stratospherically above the peso.

Went to the British Embassy a couple of times to see if there were any letters, but nothing for me. Security is so strict now, the ambassador can't sleep in the same place two nights in a row; they seem to lead a nightmare life. Even walking in the streets, you suddenly see a woman getting out of her car to go into a shop, surrounded by menacing looking men with dark glasses and bulging pockets who hover round until she comes out. Worse than that, is coming across someone being bundled into a car, screaming.

It seems most men carry a gun, so no one dares interfere when something horrible happens.

I sat in a small downtown café watching a blind couple laughing together. They looked happy. Old men tried to hawk their tatty plastic pens. One had a son in Manchester and told me he loved me. Others leered.

Letter

Had lunch in a private club in the centre of BA with a lovely young Argentine couple, Michael and Annette Corbett. Many of the old family names are British or Irish, and people speak perfect English, appearing more English than we are. It's extraordinary. They're in their thirties, glamorous and vivacious. She's got long blonde hair, with long legs to match. He is chubby, soft-spoken with dreamy, sleepy eyes, and talked to me at length about the situation here, how a military takeover is the only way to stop terrorism. They are living in a constant state of tension. He says the wealth is due to huge amounts of black money that people simply spend on non-traceable things – like boats and jewellery.

As if to prove it, Annette took me off shopping: to her jeweller where she buys gold bracelets, and to a shop like Asprey to buy wedding presents.

It was fun, but when I'm on my own, men in the streets hiss and lech at me.

I was so dazzled by the people I met and the life I was introduced to, that I failed to properly understand the gravity of the political situation. Poverty and fear were around every corner, but so was extraordinary opulence. I was staying in the centre of a sophisticated city, in houses employing maids and gardeners in uniform, with whom I spoke, went to colourful markets, laughed and discussed their families, but ultimately gleaned little of what their lives were like when they went home in the evening.

Journal

Can't get over how well the rich here live. How debauched/affluent life is. So much of everything to eat and drink, and all so cheap. The first country like this I've ever seen. They live for today, let tomorrow bring whatever it may. It feels superficial after Chile – though fun.

Invited to lunch with Isabelle and Alfredo Harrington, famous in the polo world having captained the Argentine team for years, I discovered a charming couple in their eighties, twinkling blue eyes, impeccable English, his with a strong Irish accent. He regaled me with stories of his friendship with Prince Philip, of how he'd given him his best polo mare, and had a telegram when she dropped her first foal. How Scotland Yard had cordoned off an entire area in the city when PP came to dinner with them. He was renowned for having the best polo ponies in the country, sought after especially by Americans and Australians. Having excitedly accepted their invitation to stay in the country, Alfredo asked me whether I rode astride or side-saddle. I hadn't been on a horse for an inordinately long time. He had set the bar terrifyingly high.

On the appointed morning, I appeared back at their flat, greeted by a butler to help with my small bag, a chef to offer coffee and biscuits. Alfredo looked dapper in tweeds, Isabelle in smart country clothes, and they told me more stories as we waited a long while for the driver to arrive, delayed due to an ongoing petrol strike.

Journal

Driven northwest along the Pan-American Highway past countless lovely estancias, acres of maize, herds of cattle and horses. The famous pampas are lovely. There are many Irish landowners who came over in the 1850s to get away from Protestant bullying in Ireland and settled here.

Isabelle is snappy and sweet, with a wonderful sense of humour. They are so alive and unspoilt by the grandeur in which they live.

A long, tree-lined drive led to an attractive house, where fluent-English-speaking housekeeper, butler and cook greeted us. I was hurried off to the stables where grooms in baggy trousers tucked into boots, gaucho hats, flowing scarves and knives hanging off wide belts were waiting to pay their respects. In fear and trepidation I clambered onto a large filly called Pecas, or Freckles. A groom came with me for a test ride, demonstrating how to hold the reins only in my left hand, unlike two hands at home. Legs flapping, we set off, *galopando*, and I felt as if I was wearing someone else's diamond brooch, terrified in case something should happen to it. Within half an hour I was puce in the face, sweating and exhausted. Freckles kept stopping, frantically calling her friends, while I tried to remember to keep the reins loose or she went backwards. Alfredo was not impressed.

Lunches and dinners were entirely home-grown; duck à l'orange, beef, chicken, all the fruits and vegetables one could dream of. Precisely laid-out gardens were filled with flowers, lawns mown to within an inch of their short lives. There were also seven polo pitches, with matches played throughout each day. The sky buzzed, as players came and went in small aeroplanes, still an amazement to me. They were glamorous in long boots, dark hair and perfect figures, yet somehow less appealing close up. As exotic-looking grooms waited with their ponies under the shade of enormous trees, a marvellous old groundsman barked orders at everyone. Heat was intense, the pampas stretched out to infinity, overlooked by a disproportionately vast sky packed with pale clouds.

Alfredo explained the nuances of polo, how it was much more popular than football. He used to umpire for the big international matches at Windsor and Cowdray, and in the United States. Recently, when he and Isabelle went to renew their passports in Buenos Aires, they were arrested for nightclub fraud, an unlikely scenario, a mix-up of names, and probably an attempt to extort money out of them. He kissed me goodnight on both cheeks, and then in the middle. Cheeky chap.

Letter

As almost everyone I meet socially here seems remarkably affluent, they frequently come to Europe, so I won't be saying goodbye for long, whereas in Chile, people can't afford to travel much now. I've been extraordinarily spoilt. Sitting in the dark of another power cut, Raymundo, the lovely, chubby, jolly Chilean I'm staying with in BA, tells me more stories about the chaos and wealth here, and how most people just don't realise or appreciate it.

Managed to change dollars on the black market, four times the official rate, which obviously makes everything much more reasonable. It's a paradise country if you have Green Beans, and you're not likely to be kidnapped.

Ever since I'd left Chile, I had butterflies in my stomach and couldn't stop thinking about the Anglo-Chilean man I had met at dinner: Stephen, with his aquiline face and expressive dark eyes, divorced and fed up with the narrowness of British life. We had immediately recognised each other, and although I thought him old, I found him magnetically attractive. It hadn't been easy to find time for just the two of us to meet; there were always others around. And so, he assured me he would come to Buenos Aires and find me there.

Hard as I tried not to think about him, I jumped every time the telephone in the house rang, dejected when it wasn't him. I hurried home each day hoping for a message, but there never was one. I found myself dreaming of him, and desperately tried to push those images right out of reach, but back they came. Why can't you choose who barges into your heart, I wondered, why should he appear when there is almost no chance of it going any further?

Then the telephone rang.

Of course I cancelled plans for lunch and dinner with new friends more my own age, and hurried nervously to Las Cabanas, a famous restaurant, where he was waiting. Frustratingly attractive, he asked me to drive back with him in the new car he'd come to collect. He asked again if I would like to live in Chile. How much he loved talking to me. I said nothing. He picked up my hand and studied it. I blushed and still said nothing. Another crossroads, although in my heart I knew I would continue this trip as planned, and maybe one day… We went to the cinema downtown and watched *Amarcord*, directed by Federico Fellini, in Italian with Spanish subtitles. It was like a sentence without any punctuation, sensitive and overflowing with tiny details. We went on to dinner, and then to drink pisco sours in a bar. I was dizzy with the enormity of being with him, knowing that time was running out. He said he would find me in England, although I had no address there. He was absolutely certain we would meet again.

We never did. But those butterflies flew around in my stomach for a long while.

I watched several forgettable films, good for my Spanish, and tempting, as a seat in the cinema cost 7p. When I came home one day Patricia, my host, burst out laughing as she handed me *Para Ti*, a popular fashion magazine. Inside was a photograph of me, with a score of six out of ten for the latest autumn fashion. The handkerchief covering my dirty hair was '*el último*' in style, as was the T-shirt worn over my shirt.

I kept wanting to put exclamation marks in my journal, and in my letters, but having just finished reading *Beloved Infidel*, by Sheilah Graham, I took to heart what Scott Fitzgerald told her, that using them was like laughing at your own jokes. They patronise your reader. From that moment on I avoided them.

The Corbetts invited me to stay in the campo, their enormous country house in the province of Córdoba, but their plane was 'only' a six seater, and the entire family was going: no room for me, or for the three others they had also invited. So, in the overcrowded Retiro station, I hunted for the train to Vicuña Mackenna, and then for the seat I had queued to book the previous day. Not quite enough space for any of us, two men sat opposite, listening to a football match, holding the hissing radio between them, chuckling as we spent our time shuffling feet, trying to get out of each other's way, before finally settling down to doze.

Journal

Dawn never seemed to break, and it could have been midnight at 7am, when we stopped in mist and frost at Vicuña Mackenna, where we struggled out onto the grass, across a ploughed field and bundled into a white pickup truck with 'Corbett Hermanos' painted on the sides. Driven by Matthew, a red-headed Englishman working here before he goes to Cambridge, we sped along the sand track for an hour and a half to reach Capitán Sarmiento, Michael and Annette's family home in the middle of the pampas. A sprawling white house with corrugated red roof greeted us, surrounded by immaculate lawns. Inside it reminds me of baronial Scotland, all big rooms, log fires and comfortable sofas, bowls of roses on every table, family portraits gazing down. Steaming coffee and home-cured bacon for breakfast, as Michael with his big, innocent eyes came in to welcome us, followed by Annette, their girls, and hopeful Labradors.

Although groggy after a sleepless night, I joined the eldest daughter, Yvonne, for a walk to see newborn foals. Surrounded by horses, she told me they give each of the workers seven or eight to keep for themselves. Before long I was up high on a palomino, cushioned on a sheepskin rug like an armchair, galloping across the plains. We stopped to watch hundreds of parrots flying around the trees, firework-bright in their yellows, greens and reds; we slalomed round tufts of tall silvery-white pampas grass, protected by a posse of dogs bounding alongside. Gauchos were rounding up cattle, loose horses hurried over to see us and to follow for a while. It was wonderful.

Tea of home-grown honey and scones, then a piping hot bath before two allergic-making men arrived for dinner – an architect with a too-loud, self-confident laugh, and his brother-in-law who has something I can't pinpoint, but is deeply unattractive. We all huddled by the fire. It's winter now, and seriously cold. I'm writing this by candlelight, as the electricity goes off at 11pm.

Letter

After a delicious breakfast of homemade everything, I went with Annette in the pickup to Villa Valerieste, the local pueblo. We roared along a track as wide as a motorway, and sandy as the Sahara. Leaving avenues of eucalyptus round Sarmiento, we emerged into the truly wild pampas. Flat as far as we could see, with a hot wind blowing swirls of dust into the massive sky. Dramatic, but not appealing.

The small town is surprisingly smart, nice houses, well-dressed people, all of whom appear to have English names, English voices and yet most of them have never been to Europe. It seems their grandparents settled here, and they have preserved a British way of life ever since, tuning in to the BBC World Service every night, talking about leagues instead of miles. We went into the general store, which sells everything from tapioca to loo seats, and ordered boxes of screws, tea, candles, dusters. The baker filled our sack with fresh loaves, still hot from the oven, and it took all my willpower not to rip into it on the way home, as it sat on the seat next to me smelling sublime.

We visited several old Anglo-Argentines; Fred had just electrocuted himself on a lawnmower. A strange little community out in the middle of nowhere.

Back at the ranch, while the sun was high, the girls went out on horses, galloping several miles to the corral, where gauchos were branding calves. We watched them lasso each calf, drag it into a pen, tag the ears, then castrate them. Dust hovered like red mist, covering the age-old sight with a filter, as shafts of sunlight pierced their way through, rendering the scene into a biblical painting. We helped herd the cattle into different fields, before galloping all the way home amongst the gauchos as their working day faded. One was breaking in a young horse, which danced dangerously, skittishly colliding into us; another had a delicate antique cart pulled by two fast-trotting horses. An unforgettable sight of long scarves flying, dust billowing and pounding hooves.

Letter

I've learned so much about all the work involved in raising my steak, and although it's terrible to think that these little animals are reared to be slaughtered, I'm afraid it doesn't make me love meat, or leather, any the less. It's just too good.

Journal

Lunch was a huge *asada* – lamb cooked outside on a grill, over an open fire, after which I lay for a long while by the embers, reading, dreaming, absorbed by the kindness and generosity that enveloped me.

Joined Annette to visit the miniscule village of Villa Sarmiento: three pubs and a tiny prison. We dropped supplies off at the little school, and on in the pickup to the river. Smooth-flowing, bitter-chocolate dark, surrounded by tall fluffy pampas grass and scrubby green shrubs, it was alive with birds. Matthew was with us in a red poncho, and sang quietly as we collected wood to boil the kettle for maté, a traditional South American tea made with fresh herbs, drunk on every street corner. We sat on upturned boxes, sipping the burning, bitter concoction from the dried shell of a gourd, through silver straws with a sieve on the end, watching the sun setting over immense plains, sky filled with soft pink clouds. No one said a word, there was no need.

That evening was agony: Tito and Nora came to dinner, along with ex-RAF pilot Roland and a large, plain woman called Helen. The effort to stay awake was almost impossible; to be enthusiastic and to talk, out of the question. They were perfectly nice and remarkably dull. I had become, or perhaps always had been, lazy, and probably arrogant, about talking to people I assumed wouldn't be of interest. They droned on while I drank endless cups of coffee, and hours later, conversation exhausted, still they wouldn't go. Keeping my eyes open was an unparalleled struggle. I wanted to fall down and sleep for ever. Roland thought Jamaica was in Central America, so off we went again, until saved by the lights flickering, their signal alerting us that they were about to shut down, and finally the guests said reluctant goodbyes. I may have managed to read one page of Somerset Maugham's *The Razor's Edge*, by candlelight, before falling asleep.

Days were filled with long rides, checking cattle dips and complex gate systems, watching polo from the roofs of vans on neighbouring pitches, where two brothers, each top-scoring ten-goal handicaps, lived and practised with their gaucho grooms. We were riveted, as they tried out new young ponies with electrifying speed; fun to see polo played in jeans in its natural surroundings, and realise why Argentinians are so good. These men could afford to do little else, but play. This was where the famous Santa Ana team came from. There was never a year they didn't reach the finals of many competitions, and each home match was watched by locals in rows of trucks, unlike the scores of aeroplanes lined up elsewhere.

One morning we rode fifteen kilometres, or seven leagues, as we were told, to the neighbouring estate, owned by Germans called Krups. They had introduced two zebras ten years earlier, and now had eighteen, completely wild, and looking entirely at home in country I imagined looked just like Africa. It wouldn't have surprised me to see a giraffe or elephant lumbering through the long grass.

Journal

Out across the fields to join Tito shuffling around by the cattle corral, speaking like a machine gun, where we waited for the ex-butcher, now local landlord, to come and part cattle. This is choosing which he'll buy for baby beef to be slaughtered, and which he'll leave. Each bullock is sent through a wooden alley, with sluice gates opening left or right depending on which he chose. Interesting to watch and sad to know their fate. A beautiful sun was setting in the background, turning soft clouds yellow then pink and mauve. It seemed to sink so fast. Dust flying. I can understand why people born here have such a deep affinity with the landscape. Bewitching drive back to Sarmiento, past combines finished with harvesting here, now moving on, past hares running, and eventually up the eucalyptus avenue exuding the full force of its powerful perfume.

I love sitting in the panelled room by the fire, listening to the grandfather clock ticking our lives away, bowls of roses dropping pale petals on polished mahogany tables. I'm back in another century where recent history hasn't been born. It's tranquil, thoughts provoking hopes and dreams. Out of nowhere obvious, thoughts of Federico in El Salvador butted in, how I'd like to know him better one day, and to give him an English accent better suited to his jet-set lifestyle.

'*Jeunesse ne dure qu'un moment*' according to Somerset Maugham, whose prose seems aimed directly at me.

The autumnal evenings encouraged medleys of noisy birdsong, armadillos scuffled through undergrowth, wispy clouds in the vastness of the sky. Space. Stars. Silence.

Journal

Long walk alone with the dogs. Plovers, butterflies, screeching parrots and real happiness. Tried to fathom what life is for. Reflecting on all my travels, I know it's the beauty of nature from which I've gained the most. Too late humans will learn that we're destroying ourselves by wrecking the natural world. I don't know myself well; even after twenty-two years, I'm still surprised at my reactions, but I am aware of other people's unawareness, and critical too.

Life is far too short, and I'm intensely sad this is my last day here. The verse of Lorenzo de' Medici's poem, learned when I lived in Florence years ago, still fills my head:

Quant'è bella giovinezza
che si fugge tuttavia!
Chi vuole esser lieto, sia,
di doman non c'è certezza.

Which roughly translates as:

How beautiful is youth, how fast it vanishes. If you want to be free, go for it now, there is no certainty of tomorrow.

Lorenzo died in 1492 aged forty-three.

Journal

I squeezed into the pickup with dear old Carmen, the housekeeper, witless Alberto driving, and the extremely handsome gaucho who rides steers, in Gucci shoes, behind. They dropped me off in Villa Valeria where I caught a small train to Laboulaye. There I jumped out and waited four hours for the next train, sitting on a bench in the shade of a large plane tree, though alas downwind of the men's loo. Immersed in Alan Moorehead's book, *Darwin and the Beagle*, stories of Jemmy Button, York Minster and Fuegia Basket, who, having been kidnapped and brought to Britain, were eventually returned to Tierra del Fuego to resume their natural lives, I was driven off by the stench, until the long-distance four-carriage train rattled in, and ten hours later crawled in to Buenos Aires.

As I watched light and shadow exchanging places, I wanted never to have had to leave, to have somehow preserved the exquisitely unconditional generous life I'd been lent; and I wondered if it would be harder to make my own way again.

Tension was palpable in the city. The head of the army resigned, and everyone worried it was the start of even more unrest and upheaval. I stayed in the Corbetts' large family house, still the parties continued, magicians, bitchy conversations, backbiting, unwanted wandering hands, interesting discussions, opera, sugarcane syrup with lemon and honey. Rain so relentless I couldn't go out, and men

I had met kidnapped. Elena the maid dropped an iron on her foot which swelled up so badly she was given the day off. I curled up with *Summer of the Red Wolf* by Morris West, finding BA social life had become too gossipy and petty.

Letter

There was a big shoot-up just outside the gates of the house last night, but not a trace of anything this morning. A friend is helping the wife and children of a man who's been kidnapped, and not a word heard in the six months since it happened.

I was taken to a British Community showing of BBC wildlife documentaries on Argentina, where at least two hundred dreary-looking people, all very jolly and thrilled to see each other, wittered in a camaraderie of expat collusion. I was wincing, trying to convince myself that English people aren't really like that. But after eight months away, I'm beginning to wonder. The films were fabulous.

Annette has lent me coats, dresses and jerseys, as the weather is suddenly bitingly cold. My only pair of jeans and poncho aren't enough, although somehow they attract attention. Having a farewell dinner with friends and all their children, they produced another monthly fashion magazine, and to my total disbelief, there was another picture of me, looking into a shop window, oblivious to the photograph being taken. Under the title 'Latest Autumn Fashion, What Elegant People are Wearing in the Streets of BA on a Day that is Hot but could turn Cold', there I was in my same scruffy jeans with the same T-shirt over a shirt, a spotty handkerchief on my head, which they praised as the *último* in chic. We all cried with laughter, and at the sadness of saying goodbye.

Amongst the generosity of farewell dinners with so many friends was the problem of actually leaving. Next up was Paraguay, but the Argentine government brought out a new law that all foreigners had to buy travel tickets with dollars. I had none, and as no bank would sell any, that was an impossibility. Annette's long-suffering and well-connected brother contacted the director of the bus company, and managed to fix the ticket problem. By which time the Paraguayan border had closed for political reasons, so I still couldn't leave.

More superfluous days filled with reading, walking and cinema. I saw *The Odessa File*, disappointing having read the book, so much was left out. I climbed high into the cheapest seats of the Teatro Colón to listen to Mozart and Schubert. They were days in limbo. My subconscious had already moved on, but I was still being entertained and looked after. I'd encountered such overwhelming kindness, but their world seemed gradually to shrink and tighten like a clamp around me.

Without warning the border opened, and I joined a long queue of Paraguayans and Mormons jostling in the fume-filled terminal for the first bus heading to Paraguay. 'You've had it, chum,' said Annette as we hugged, the lump in my throat dissolving into tears as I finally waved adieu to a large group of friends who had also turned up to send me on my way. It had been a long, emotional farewell to an unforgettable and extraordinary few weeks.

A SLIVER OF PARAGUAY

Have You Ever Seen The Rain

The long-distance bus, apparently a Rápido model, took twenty-four hours to roll into Asunción, the capital of Paraguay. A voluptuous hostess on board in a short, tight skirt dished out plastic trays filled with soggy paper cups of revolting sweet coffee, thick with tinned milk, and an inexhaustible supply of doorstop sandwiches: fat, dry white bread smeared with a little grease and lurid pink meat, all of which I consumed. Inertia was imminent. Next came *gaseosa* drinks in high-vis colours, while outside the sun set over low hills, scrubby trees shaped like sinister figures, silhouettes in black against the flaming sky.

An old woman next to me chewed on a fat cigar, took off her shoes and tightened her headscarf under her chin, folded like the Queen's.

Fluffy clouds vanished into the darkness as we all settled onto our hard seats to doze with our dreams, before shuffling out again at numerous stops until we reached the border with Paraguay.

Letter

Customs checks were the worst of all thirteen countries I've been through. Made to open our bags in the mud, sweat trickling down my face in sudden humidity. Twice they rifled through every single thing with grubby fingers, but thank God took nothing. Many of the passengers had the most innocent things taken away. That was leaving Argentina.

A ferry to Paraná across the river to the Paraguay customs who repeated the same performance: mud, a salacious scrummage through everything, wave of a filthy hand, and all of a sudden out and into the bus terminal in Asunción.

The small city is far more attractive than I'd imagined, with pretty colonial buildings, balustrades, wrought iron, stone carvings and numerous parks. With only a million inhabitants it feels tiny, but sadly rain was belting down and had turned the streets into a running muddy mess. The floods in Argentina and here have been relentless, and swathes of the countryside are impassable, with roads closed, cattle isolated and farms underwater.

I found a sleazy room for the night, no lights working, otherwise good enough. The river outside my window was rising fast, alive with cargo boats, and land flat as far as I could see. It felt like somewhere East, jungle, tropical, something of the surrounding areas of Guayaquil, Graham Greene country.

Guarani is spoken as much as Spanish, the currency is in guaranis, and although clearly a poor country, there are, as ever, Mercedes and fat American cars in the streets. And time has somehow lost an hour between here and Argentina.

Morning brought no respite from the rain, and I decided to move on towards Brazil, struggling with my heavy case through the mud and back to the terminal. Buses were abandoned like stranded beetles, thick mud coating their rusty bodies. Few people were around, and I was surprised to find my bus, engine revving, ready to leave. It was almost empty, save for a nosy, corpulent Paraguayan with a dejected-looking American couple under her chubby arm. She flung questions at me in guttural Spanish, fingers pointing, demanding answers. 'Where you go? What your country? What you do?' The only other passenger, a middle-aged bearded Australian, was, thank goodness, monosyllabic.

As we sloshed through the streets of Asunción, causing waves of mud to batter brick walls protecting houses with their gardens of tropical flowers, I felt curiously ill at ease looking into the privacy of homes from my elevated, sagging bus seat. Then with no punctuation, we were passing desolate, poor, small shacks which must have been flooded through with our wash of muddy water. These small dwellings now sported tiled roofs, like wonky hats, instead of the ubiquitous Argentine tin; a sense of somewhere like Nicaragua, banana groves, cotton and coffee plantations, gaggles of strong, thin men with scythes cutting sodden grass. It was both familiar and strange to be back in the tropics, elegant coconut palms reaching up to touch the sky, Brahman cattle following each other with saggy jowls and humpy backs.

We passed the village of Itauguá, famous for weaving lace, dirty pieces of which were festooned across buildings in a bid to lure us in. But soon the deep red muddy puddles across the road splattered up and coated the coach windows, leaving me in the dark in every way. I mentally put Paraguay last on my list as a place to live. Perhaps on a par with Honduras. Even now that it was June, and winter, it felt humid and unpleasant, although to be fair I hadn't given it much of a chance.

MUSIC, MAGNIFICENCE AND A TRAIN ROBBER IN BRAZIL

The Girl From Ipanema
La Bamba

The tired, ramshackle bus limped over the border from Paraguay, and without a wave of a hand, let alone a baggage check, we had left Spanish-speaking Latin America behind, and were through into Brazil, my fourteenth country. I knew this was likely to be the last official stamp I'd have pressed into my passport for a long while. In the annals of well-known rhymes, the ditty from travelling son to his father goes, 'No mon, No fun, Love Son'. To which the reply comes back, 'So sad, Too bad, Love Dad'. I had almost run out of funds, and was now in a country whose language is Portuguese. I had spoken Spanish for the past eight months, was dreaming in Spanish and could happily communicate wherever I went. Although accents had varied and vocabularies changed, I had always felt at ease with those around me. Now I was stumped. I tried speaking slowly in Spanish, and occasionally a long-suffering Brazilian had the patience to speak even more slowly, so we could grasp a semblance of a conversation.

The bus trundled on into Foz do Iguaçu, a muddy, dirty, thriving little town, springboard for the mighty Iguaçu Falls, where I squeezed into a minibus with other stragglers making our way to the famous *cataratas*. The lumpy, bumpy countryside was an overflowing jungle of greens; palm trees, ferns and creepers; an intense contrast to the plains of Argentina, and as we rounded another bend, a shout went up as the vast Iguaçu River, way down below, came into view, frothing and broiling as it gathered itself together again after hurtling over the famous falls.

I untangled myself from the detritus of backpacks, dragged my too-heavy broken red suitcase from the roof and brazenly staggered into the smart pink and white colonial building of the Cataratas Hotel, where a bellboy took my tatty luggage into the foyer without a word. And in the full-length mirror of the ladies' loo, I caught sight of a scruffy scarecrow with wild hair and bags under her eyes.

Letter

They are the largest broken falls in the world, in a wonderful, remote setting. Twice the width and water volume of Niagara and about one hundred feet higher, deep in the jungle, straddling the border with Brazil, Argentina and Paraguay. Rickety platforms and paths are built around the different cascades which make up the whole, so you can creep along and gaze right down at the foaming mass, or up at the torrents of water thundering down. There are over 270 different falls, and as you slither along the wet walkways, covered in spray, hundreds of bright butterflies the size of plates flap past. They are black and white with purple Art Nouveau swirls, velvety reds, blues the colour of night, and all around diminutive turquoise birds chatter, as parakeets and budgerigars chase brightly coloured insects into dense undergrowth. This is the most phenomenal place.

Journal

I crept around a corner and found myself over the Devil's Throat fall. Following one pitch, tumbling, spilling, surging from the top down, reminded me of slo-mo photography. Hypnotic and deeply, powerfully impressive. I could see people on the Argentine side navigating their walkways, wearing hired yellow oilskins to offset the worst of the spray. Decided I couldn't afford to rent one, and have only eaten fruit today, so feeling wet and wobbly.

I explored the exquisite hotel, tiptoeing around a voluminous swimming pool overlooked by an aviary of parrots, gaping through windows into smart dark rooms, once more passing the bellboy who, seeing me struggling, carried my case right down to the bus stop. I didn't have money to tip him. Felt bad. Last long look at the widest falls, and at the beautiful cascading white water, while a setting sun burnt clouds into a dusky sky.

That night in a family-filled house was clean and cosy, but £1.20 for a heaped plate of Milanesa, salad and rice was more expensive than any other country. By torchlight I added another squiggle on my map of Latin America, and wondered how much longer I could continue this self-indulgent, itinerant way of life.

An insistent morning roused me, music and raucous birdsong filtered through dreams, and as I watched this new world from my window, with its different language and vegetation, I temporarily discarded financial fears and relished once more the remarkable kindness to an outsider. Bruno refused to charge for my breakfast of rolls with coffee, and Rosa, who owned the room I slept in, offered me another night for free. Generosity from people who had little themselves always stabbed me into a guilty, grateful introspection. I was so damned lucky.

Hitching a ride back to the falls in a truck filled with grinning road builders, this morning they seemed even more impressive. Myriads of rainbows shimmered, caught between sunshine and spray, mesmerising power and force of water. And all the time smells of the forest, the after-rain, from so many trees, creepers and exotic flowers.

Journal

I sat right at the front of the bus to São Paulo, partitioned by glass from the drivers who wouldn't stop staring at me. All the way. A couple of Japanese sat behind, talking, as far as I was concerned, incomprehensibly at each other, taking their shoes on and off and giggling hysterically. We stopped at countless tiny villages until the bus was full, and finally rumbled, uninterrupted, through the dark. A fitful, draughty night and still the lecherous drivers continued to stare.

Picture-book high, thick jungle on all sides as the sun came up, rain stopped and clouds dispersed. We stopped for a breakfast of yoghurt, and the usual delicious strong, hot, free coffee. Brazilian loos are the best so far, all of them immaculate, but despite the caffeine, I struggled to keep my eyes open for the rest of the journey. Eyelids weighted down and padlocked shut, prised open occasionally as we tore along, in time to notice small settlements and farms, plantations of bananas, coffee and fruit, hacked out of the jungle. Rivers meandered into lakes, men with universal scythes slashed at overgrown verges. It was all a blur of twisted greens, sinewy tree trunks, punctuated by a few shacks, causing a serious conflict with my critical self. Sleep was winning, and I woke with a dry mouth, cracked lips and aching body to find the bus surrounded by characterless steel and glass skyscrapers, thick traffic and only the faintest glimpse of a blue sky in the heart of São Paulo.

Letter

Brazil claims the prize for being by far the most exorbitant country I've been in, which is no joke now. An orange, grown by the ton all year round, costs the equivalent of 5p. The country is booming, the currency strong and the dollar worth little. São Paulo is exactly as I imagine New York to be: skyscrapers, a population of eight million that increases by half a million each year, hellish pollution, with traffic jams in every street. I can't yet see its charm.

Forcing limbs, stiff from being in one uncomfortable position for too long, into a kind of shuffle-stagger, dazed from lack of sleep, I pushed my way through almost impenetrable crowds thronging the vast São Paulo bus terminal, in search of a public telephone. '*Telefono*? *Telefono*?' I squawked to everyone. Eventually an elderly man dragging a heavy box on a string behind him pointed vaguely to the right, and pushed me across the human tide to reach the other side. There were three black telephones on short strings attached to boxes for money.

I waited while people in front of me made calls, screamed into the receiver, dropped their coins, scrabbled in pockets for numbers, jostled each other, until finally it was my turn. I was nervous: about to ring the Brazilian family who had been on the same boat exploring the Galápagos Islands, whom I hadn't been in touch with since. Dolores had said as we triple-kissed goodbye all those months ago that I should definitely stay with them if I made it as far as São Paulo. Well, here I was with nothing to lose. I pushed the coins into their slot, waited while they slid down, dialled the long number she had given me, and waited again. It rang, sounding like a klaxon deep inside my ear, and was answered by a maid who miraculously understood my tremulous voice, as I asked for the Senhora. Dolores was not only there, but immediately insisted I come and stay with them, and before long I was in a small red VW taxi heading to a residential area of the huge city.

The house was big, filled with dark furniture and rambling rooms. It sat in the middle of a large garden edged with palm trees, behind which sculptures of naked nymphs and frolicking dolphins peered out. Neon lighting completed the stage-set experience. I thought it hideous, but was overcome with gratitude, tinged with guilt, that they were having me to stay. Apart from the family, it was home to six maids, two gardeners, a chauffeur and their pilot. Dolores admitted she couldn't remember exactly who I was from the boat trip, but treated me as part of the family anyway. Her auburn hair, greying at the roots, was swept into a neat ponytail; a sweet, generous smile; she wore jeans tucked into boots, her outsize shirt hiding, perhaps, a little extra weight gained since we had last met.

After scrubbing away the stale smells of my long bus journey, we settled down to a lunch of fresh tangerine juice, papayas and cheeses from their farm, salads with delicious, curious vegetables I had never seen before, followed by pumpkin and coconut sweets. The little girls, Susanna and Helene, had grown; shy, complex Jacques hugged me tight, his shoulders broader, his torso taller than before, still his hair longer than his sisters'. Dolores later told me of his problems, how he saw a psychiatrist every day, her worries and concerns for his life. 'He can't stick with anything. He starts a course, then quits.'

Daughter Grace was in Rio with their father Alberto, whom I had yet to meet. His brother was governor of São Paulo, his sister famous, although why I had no idea. He, Alberto, owned the largest record company in Brazil, had several farms and copious other businesses. He had clearly made a comfortable life for himself.

Dolores and the girls treated me like a long-lost member of the family, and even though I ached with cold as winter evenings closed in, I slept dreamlessly in the shared bedroom with Helene, Isabella and their platoons of teddies lined up along my bed. I had tossed the dice, and fickle-fingered fate was once more looking after me.

The flower market was flanked by lorries filled to overflowing with fresh bounty: banks of lilies, ferns, roses of all shapes and colours, spiky flaming-orange petals on stems whose names I didn't know, gladioli and a thousand varieties of exotic tropical flowers. Men in suits bartered with stall holders, maids in uniforms ordered enormous arrangements. Dolores bought a dull box of green things for the office and whisked us back for lunch in her sports car. She was trying out a new cook for one of the farms, whose food turned out to be a triumph of creativity. We slavered over her delicate little pastries deftly filled with prawns and beans, or meat and herbs, followed by avocado ice cream. I had never eaten an avocado other than savoury, and this sweet variation opened up a whole new world of possibilities. Soon, I was drinking frothy, thick avocado milkshakes sweetened with honey, seasoned with lemon juice, on a daily basis, not giving a moment's thought to the calorific intake.

Carlos, the driver, took me to his favourite place, the Snake Museum, where I watched in horror and fascination as each glass cage contained another nightmarish serpent. There were anacondas, boa constrictors, rattlesnakes, coral snakes, vipers. Many were flickering their tongues in and out as they slithered through grass, curled round rocks and reared their heads at pink rats darting about, scampering for their lives. Not for long. A man was milking a cobra, extracting venom by squeezing the back of its head with tweezers. He dropped a rattlesnake on the floor and let it slide around, before handing out harmless coral snakes to anyone who wanted to hold one. Then came the spiders, vast black hairy things, tiny vicious black widows. All too creepy and nasty for me to take any longer, I fled home and bumped straight into Alberto.

I was instantly beguiled by this tall, handsome man. His voice was soft; long fair hair and deep blue eyes that stared unblinking into mine. He observed me too closely. Thoughtful and sensitive, his charm immediately wrapped me up and rendered me blushing and stuttering.

After dinners of palm heart soup, or giant prawns grilled, crunchy on the outside, flesh soft, pink and delicate inside, or fish in unfamiliar, tangy sauces, mouth-watering crèmes caramels with sauces of dulce de leche, I was pressed to eat little treats made from papaya and coconut, while Alberto regaled me with stories. I learned about his record company, his street-sweeping machines, his farms, his views on the mentality of Brazilian people. We listened to a new long-playing record by his friend Ney Matogrosso, performing in a drag show in Rio at that moment.

He and Dolores were gracious and relaxed with me, and yet I felt awkward being a stranger in their midst. Jacques occasionally came into the room, tossed his long mane, announcing he was off to the beach for the weekend to surf, and shimmied out. He considered I had sided with the enemy, and no longer emptied his convoluted feelings at me.

A visit to the record factory, with Dolores and the girls, felt like landing on a different planet. I was speechless as we wandered through a monumental state-of-the-art structure of glass and steel, light and airy, filled with the latest equipment from North America: computers, gargantuan blocks of flashing lights and buttons, telex machines which clunked and whirred, spewing out ribbons of encrypted paper, desks lost under tangled telephones and files.

Journal

Alberto insisted I choose some LPs from the giant storeroom to drag back to England, and so I lurched out, thrilled, under the weight of Roberta Flack, Carly Simon, Neil Diamond, Aretha Franklin, Ney Matogrosso and several other Brazilian artists.

During another scrumptious lunch, he abruptly stood up and said, 'Pack. We're going to the farm.' I pushed my toothbrush into a pocket, and the three of us roared to the airport and into their six-seater plane. I have never been in a small one before, and was tense as we took off in such a tiny machine over the vast city, but as soon as I got used to bouncing up and down in the air pockets, I loved it, and peered down on coffee plantations, cotton, oranges, sugarcane, woods of eucalyptus, and over the hilly countryside with its rivers and lakes. And then, all of a sudden, we veered sideways, tilted sharply downwards, and landed on the tufty grass runway of the farm.

Diana and Scott, the Gordon setters from a Mrs Richmond in England, came bouncing to meet us, black and tan, hair silky and shiny in the bright sunlight. A car was immediately on its way to collect the bags while we walked, the dogs barking with delight, leaping alongside. The house is beautiful with a lovely sense of calm, designed by Alberto and Dolores. Arches, high ceilings and cavernous rooms filled with old artefacts they've collected; ancient pitchforks, baskets, pitchers, chests and benches.

Each evening Alberto played his guitar on the terrace while we drank pisco sours and mojitos under the spotlight of an almost full moon. As the cold night air slid penetratingly under our outsize shawls, we wandered inside to be thawed by a blazing, crackling fire, flames alive, warming, spitting, radiating life. We nibbled home-produced cheeses, nuts and pastries, our glasses were changed and filled with wine. Alberto put his guitar to one side and told me stories of Brazil. From the destructive giant ants to contemporary architecture. How to treat a snakebite and how to dance samba. He was fervently pro the current government, explaining how they were developing the country, giving people incentives of tax relief. He was convinced 'they have the right ideas and are forging the country ahead. It's booming'. It was not for me to question his convictions. I bit my lip and remained silent, sceptical at his contradictions; his halting English was peppered with 'It's a mess. A total mess.'

Exploring the orchards with Dolores, we picked lemons, limes, oranges, and plucked round purple-black jabuticaba berries that grew directly on the trunk of the tree, giving my taste buds yet another adventure. We watched hummingbirds, their tiny wings beating so fast they created the high-pitched sound that gives them their name. Dolores told me how fierce and territorial they are, harbingers of good luck. She took me round the cotton stores and baling sheds, workers in loose turbans and baggy overalls shyly glancing up from their tasks. We walked through the coffee plantations chewing buds, sucking the sweet juice and crunching unripe beans. I was fascinated by so many crops new to me, seeing them at such close quarters. Learning.

Alberto suddenly decided he wanted to go back to São Paulo, and so we bundled fruit and vegetables together, said goodbye to the dogs, who gazed with sad, accusatory eyes, their bodies suddenly dejected. The little plane circled twice round over the farm, back up into the air pockets, where we were thrown around like leaves in a tornado, and back to the vast, rain-sodden city, which seemed somehow more daunting than ever.

Journal

Spent all afternoon talking with Alberto, who told me more about Brazil's economy, how exporting oil will change everything. He spoke about life before the 1964 revolution, the corruption and advancing communism, and now how stable life is.

'It really is the country of today and of the future, in spite of intense overcrowding and increasing populations in the big cities. That's scary, but we'll come through, and everyone will prosper.'

I'm not convinced.

He spoke about his grandmother, famous in Brazil for her social work and for founding hospitals, before switching to the yacht he wants to buy. 'You could be the cook on board,' he said to me, 'and we will sail through the South Pacific…'

Well, no thanks. Even though he's forty-two, and I'm hypnotised, that doesn't fit in with my dreams.

The end of wandering looms. I have a sinking feeling, and found a Thomas Cook agency today in case I could cash in my air ticket from Rio, battered around the edges, but still valid, red carbon paper intact. But there are no one-way cargo passages to Europe, no affordable passenger boats.

I telephoned an English friend, Ninian, living in Rio whom I hadn't seen for several years. Our parents were friends, and I had found him attractive and awkward. The line was bad, and I couldn't make out whether I could stay with him or not, whether he'd even be there. Dolores generously, and perhaps strategically, bought my bus ticket, refusing to let me pay her back. The die was cast.

I paid a final visit to the Museum of Modern Art with its strangely displayed paintings: each one sat on a glass stand with the name of the artist on the back, so one had to walk around each at least once. I marvelled again at Goya, the *Man in Black* by Velázquez, Bosch's riveting *Temptation of St. Anthony* with its monsters and freaks, and the fabulous tree full of movement and power by Soutine. I wondered how the bad portrait by Lawrence had found its way in. The list went on and I had to force myself away, back to the house to pack, after which I sat in the garden writing last-minute letters, gardeners and cooks jabbering at me unintelligibly, while the German shepherd prowled around depositing large messes over a manicured lawn.

Alberto appeared in a shockingly shiny suit to say goodbye. If I hadn't been so infatuated, that sudden aberration might have flipped my affectionate feelings for him. He was a terrible sight, suddenly a spiv, a different man to the one who wore cowboy boots and battered jeans, who had gazed at me with such intense, unwavering blue eyes. I shook hands with him, which felt even odder having become so close and talked intimately about so much during the past days. He had put on a new costume and adopted a new personality.

Dolores and I hugged, promised we would see each other in London, little knowing what life would have in store, and then I was off through shrieking traffic back to the bus terminal for a beautiful eight-hour drive to Rio.

Journal

Such a smart bus, sadly ponged out by a diminutive man sitting next to me, who reeked of unwashed body, unwashed clothes and garlic breath smothering unbrushed teeth.

A new dual carriageway swaggered up steep-sided hills, over mountains and eventually through the suburbs and industrial areas to the terminal in Rio, where I was spat out into a predictable melee of people pushing, shouting, hawking and laughing. There was no code for the chaotic human highway, as once again I shuffled my way to a payphone, trying at least twenty times to get through to Ninian. It was endlessly engaged. Eventually, as I was beginning to shed tears of frustration and anxiety, yelled at by the furious queue behind, he answered, told me to find a taxi, and gave directions to his apartment overlooking Copacabana Beach. I persuaded the wiry old taxi driver in shorts and a string vest to take me first to the British Consulate, where I could collect longed-for mail. I hadn't heard from my parents or from friends for almost two months.

Journal

We helter-skeltered around traffic through the centre of Rio, bustling with people parading suntanned flesh, thronging the streets and filling sidewalk cafés. Isolated old buildings amongst the skyscrapers seemed bravely defiant. I entrusted the driver with all my belongings, and ran into the consulate to collect letters. So excited, high on anticipation, but then such a let-down. I had three depressed ones from Ma, about the expense of living, how she can't take Pa a moment longer, and how strongly she feels about his greatest friend. That was all she wrote about. I had one from a friend of hers asking me what was going on between my parents. I read them quickly, once. And wish I hadn't seen them. My air ticket runs out in a few weeks, and quite simply, I don't want to go back.

Stepping into the vast apartment on the eighth floor of Avenida Atlântica helped blow the blues away. Ninian was waiting, blonde floppy hair, blue eyes staring unblinking at me. He was thinner than I remembered and seemed nervous. An American, Bruce, was staying with him, immediately easy, interested and attractive.

Journal

While Ninian went to concoct reviving caipirinhas in the kitchen, and to discuss dinner with Tina, his cheerful, smiling maid, I felt hollow with hunger and found it hard to concentrate as Bruce told me how Ninian said he used to have a crush on me, but that I never knew. I guess I felt the same and he never knew. Why is it that emotional communication can be so awkward? Guess I'll never realise what I've missed by being too shy to say what I really feel.

The apartment overlooked the long, beautiful bay, with its artificially wide beach, broad boulevard, palm trees and Atlantic waves rolling in. The air was warm, it felt tropical and exciting as we sat out on the balcony having dinner.

Ninian stared at me throughout, flattering, disarming, asking questions, wanting to know too much about my life. He talked in great detail about the business he had started: something to do with sterilising medical equipment, which was taking all sixty minutes of his every waking hour, determined that it would succeed.

During my stay I found him increasingly attractive. It was clearly mutual but he was rarely at home, often coming back late, exhausted, always flattering, asking me to stay on. 'You can live here. Why go back?' Indeed, I wondered that too, but my crumpled air ticket was all I had to get me over the Atlantic. Friends came round, and along with Bruce I joined them all for cocktails on the beach, relishing the fun of being amongst people more or less my own age again. The laughter, the banter, the harmless flirting. All the time I tried to ignore a weight in the pit of my stomach, the dread of returning 'home'. To what?

During the days, when Bruce and Ninian were at work, I walked along the beaches, Copacabana and on to Ipanema. They were names I knew well from songs. You could get earworms from 'The Girl From Ipanema'.

Journal

Sat on rocks and watched surfers springing lightly onto their boards, catching waves that thundered onto the sand. Every boy has long sun-bleached hair and looks like Jacques. There are fat, squidgy old men squeezed into revolting tanga Speedos, skinny ones in huge boxer shorts. Women are equally varied in shape and skin tone, and even well-endowed ancient grandmothers make me feel I'm wearing a fur coat in my normal bikini. Theirs are microscopic, and far from sunbathing, most of them seem to be doing press-ups, or physical jerks, and then running. I feel lazy simply walking along the soft sand looking at them. Two men in beach clothes came close and flashed their police badges, but only to alert me to be careful as apparently there are thieves and drug dealers preying on single women.

Reading *Jaws*, by Peter Benchley; cold, calculating and compulsive, it diverted me from feeling uneasy on the shore, but terrorised me from going into the water.

Letter

Away from the coast I explored Rio, squeezing onto crowded buses going the wrong direction, eventually finding my way to the front of a funny little cable train, so steep that I fell off the seat as we lumbered up through jungle and butterflies to the vast Art Deco statue of Cristo, standing on the peak of Corcovado, high above the city it dominates. The hunchback mountain feels as if it's exerting control over the breathtaking views of Rio, and on out to hundreds of misty islands beyond.

At the summit, scores of overweight people with wobbly tummies were overflowing small chairs, tucking into outsize steaks, or taking photographs of each other, seemingly oblivious of the extraordinary panorama below, or to the nine-metre-high Christ towering over them. Everywhere you rest your eyes, you see either sand and sea, or green hills and palm trees. I gazed down on parks, like oases encircled by old houses, on numerous lakes reflecting the palms that surround them, and down to the traffic snaking way below.

It was late when I returned one evening to the eighth floor, to find Bruce and Ninian had clearly been discussing me, and drinking. They plied me with knock-out batida, a cocktail of fruit juice and cachaça, their local firewater. Ninian told me, as he fixed me with his magnetic clear blue eyes, that we should have had an affair years ago, while Bruce discussed sex, so that soon I was shy of his flattery, embarrassed by both of them. They laughed conspiratorially. With still-warm air billowing into the room, I gazed through the open doors at the moon, the pulsating cars below, the swaying lights and the eternally swishing waves. Rio, where night was always young.

'We're going to a party with Ronnie Biggs,' Ninian said one evening, as he dumped a pile of documents on the table. His work was so consuming I wondered how he had energy to party. 'Do you remember he took part in the Great Train Robbery about ten years ago, and now he's living an hour outside Rio?'

I wasn't sure how I felt about meeting the man who had helped mastermind the theft of £2.6 million from a mail train heading from Glasgow to London in 1963, and had been given thirty years in jail. Two years later he escaped from Wandsworth Prison, having scaled a thirty-foot-high perimeter wall, jumped onto a furniture van parked outside, and had been, so far, ten years on the run. He'd had plastic surgery, acquired a new identity, new documents, and worked as a builder in Australia, where he and his wife had a third son. But he got wind that Interpol was on his tail, and escaped, via Panama and Venezuela, to Rio, where there was no extradition treaty between Britain and Brazil. There he fathered a Brazilian son, giving him an added layer of immunity.

Meanwhile the famous Detective Slipper of Scotland Yard was in pursuit and, tipped off by the *Daily Express*, to which he gave assurances that he wouldn't leak their scoop, he made a farcical, secretive and hopeless attempt to arrest Ronnie in Brazil, without telling the Home Office, Foreign Office or Brazilian authorities. His bungled handling of such a high-profile convict made headlines around the world, and caused much amusement as he was photographed returning home empty-handed.

Thus forewarned, with Ninian driving, we set off out of the city, heading for the hills, and were soon lost. Dusk embraced us, followed swiftly by a deep darkness. We stopped at isolated cafés along the roadside, hoping for guidance, met with shrugs, until eventually an old man on a bicycle with no lights was able to direct us.

By the time we arrived, the party had thinned out, but those who were left were still wandering around outside, peering in the dark to see who they'd missed. Ronnie Biggs, our host, came straight up to us, a short, good-looking man, genuinely charming, carrying his nine-month-old son. I was told by one of the guests that there had just been a publicity stunt involving the British media, focussing on the child and his young Brazilian mother. Photographs were taken of Ronnie with his bare-breasted girlfriend, of whom there was no sign this evening.

'Introduce yourselves to the others,' he said in an Estuary accent, waving his free arm.

I looked around, at an enormously tall man from Los Angeles, some famous athlete, the tallest man I had ever seen, in a baggy suit with trousers waving around his ankles. He looked like a character from a children's book. Alongside him a man in brown and white co-respondent shoes, a brown suit with white tie and trilby, stood on an upturned box. 'To see what it feels like to be this tall. Nice to meet ya, I'm from Middlesex.' A lecherous man called Joe with leery half-closed eyes that kept wandering down my shirt sidled over to chat me up. Geraldine with blonde curly hair came to look at me, but was instantly bored, and stared firmly over my shoulder to see who next to embark on. She spotted Ninian, and hurried towards him. Ronnie's large, half-built house stood behind us, lights from the open windows throwing weird-shaped shadows onto the grass.

He came over again, still holding his baby, and was happy to talk about himself. 'Yeah, I might've stayed in Caracas except they issued a warrant for my arrest, so I came here and cashed in my ticket. I can't get papers, so I can't legally work. Have to report to the Rio police twice a week. Not meant to travel, or drink or go to clubs.' He chatted on, telling me he was doing up his house, was due to celebrate ten years of freedom in a couple of months.

I asked him what he missed most about England.

'Ah,' he replied, momentarily thoughtful. 'I miss fish 'n' chips, and a cold, misty morning.' He was an amiable, even-tempered man with whom I would have liked to discuss so much more than this bonkers gathering would allow.

I struggled on, talking to whoever was there, mostly Brits from a murky underworld, all of whom were friendly, and curious to know what I was doing.

'Please can we go, I'm so sleepy,' I murmured to Ninian, who had got rid of Geraldine, extracted himself from a red-clawed cougar, and was equally ready to leave. But he had forgotten to turn the car lights off, the battery was dead, so we started to push.

Freewheeling back, down steep hills, we passed scores of little sacrificial pyres, symbolic of the Afro-Brazilian religion, macumba, lit with candles on street corners, scattered with flower petals. The sun was up – it was five in the morning.

Journal

Sunday morning. Ninian and I zipped downtown to the market bursting with hammocks, tobacco stalls, watch menders, photographers with heads under black covers, as they pressed buttons on long cords, their subjects impatient at having to pose for so long. Kebab stands, plump yellow *choclos* cooking on homemade grills, tropical flowers shoved into buckets. Smoke and smells intermingled, and all around there was music. Alive and bustling, wherever there was space people danced. N was always a hundred yards ahead, teasing and appealing. We drank delicious mixtures of avocado with passion fruit as we sauntered around, bargaining over the cost of lemons, rejecting pleas to buy birds in small cages.

Lunch at a packed bar where you could eat as much meat as you wanted: pork, steak, chicken, sausages piled high. Ninian ate so fast I could barely see the movement of fork to mouth, and couldn't begin to keep pace, leaving a plate still full as we tore out and bumped into an exhilarating, spontaneous samba on the pavement. People were drumming empty beer cans and tapping tabletops with cutlery. They shimmied, they stomped, tossing heads, butts, feet fast-moving. Whistles blew for a change of beat and rhythm. Enthralled, it was impossible not to join in and dance amongst the raucous, joyous crowd. Children whirled in a frenzy of arms and legs, a man in a yellow shirt danced sexily with a mesmerising, beautiful girl, and when the music stopped, fighting broke out. I was subjected to a leering bearded man who followed me and, when Ninian wasn't beside me, pawed at me. No one on my travels until Brazil had invaded my space quite so much or so often, and I was naively surprised at their brazenness.

From the apartment balcony, I watched as Ninian strode out of the building, lean and fit, across wide Copacabana Beach towards the sea. I waited until he'd gone into the water, before creeping downstairs in my not-so-itsy-bitsy bikini after him. Months of eating and drinking, not to mention snacking at every opportunity, had added embarrassing extra inches to every part of my body. I slunk onto a towel, burrowed down, pretending I hadn't seen him, and assumed I was invisible. But within moments a woman strode up, bent over and said in English, 'I recognise you. You're an air hostess with British Caledonian, aren't you? Tell me what people are wearing in England now?'

Self-conscious, I dozed, and woke as the day cooled, covered in ugly red sandfly bites, to find I was surrounded by men staring down at me as if they'd found an unidentifiable mythical creature. We were all bemused and silent, except for the sound of those green waves rolling in, breaking with foam onto palest sand, ensuring absolute beauty was never far away.

Days passed with visits to travel agents, still unsuccessfully pleading for a one-way boat trip to Europe. Exchange rates rose in my favour, and I bought a night-bus ticket to Ouro Preto. A blind man sat next to me, quietly humming, while his chubby friend behind talked loudly and incessantly to himself.

Journal

Woke at four when most people piled out, and watched a flamingo-pink dawn break over misty hills with mountains beyond, as the sky split to reveal a brilliant orange glow. We jolted along hilly, cultivated deep red earth, at last coming over the top to look down on to Ouro Preto, the prettiest colonial town I've seen in SA. Unified with tiled roofs and balconies, yet each house has its own character with different coloured walls and doorways. After surprising advice from the little tourist office, I knocked on a door of the synagogue and was offered a room for free. It had a bed, smelled bad, but there were students, all men studying mining and minerals, milling around, and no one seemed surprised I was there.

Letter

People have been mining gold in this area since the Portuguese colonised Brazil, and in this enchantingly picturesque town, locals are still involved with it and its tangled history of fortunes made and lives lost. I explored steep, roughly cobbled streets with numerous Rococo churches, their interiors heavy with carved golden woodwork, countless statues and dark paintings. Every narrow lane has views out to the hills beyond, revealing more churches stretching into the countryside. It seems to me that for every ounce of gold that came out of the ground religion has needed to atone.

The story of San Francisco, an ornately opulent 18th-century church, stayed in my mind long after most of the others had stirred themselves into a jumble of kaleidoscopic precious idols burdened with carving and biblical references. Much of the sculpture in San Francisco had been created by the illegitimate son of a Portuguese architect and an enslaved African, called Lisboa, who was known locally as Aleijadinho, 'the Little Cripple'.

The story went that as a result of syphilis he lost all his toes, and then his fingers fell off, leaving him with only a thumb and forefinger on each hand. The pain was so intense, he cut off the remaining fingers with his sculpting chisel, somehow continuing his exquisite work by tying his tools on to his wrists.

Food played an important part as always in my everyday life. Here, as usual, it was expensive, and I balked at paying 60p for a plate of beans, pork, rice and salad. Usually, I fended off exhaustion after a long overnight journey by eating empanadas of cheeses, grilled and wrapped in varieties of pastries, or breads depending on local customs. In Brazil, thick creamy milkshakes were offered on street corners, ubiquitous banana being the mainstay, both filling and ultimately unsatisfactory. And so, I wandered around Ouro Preto, in a haze of brief uplift from another snack, followed by a struggle to concentrate while I read about another church, or attempted to follow complex labels in the School of Mineralogy. This was a charming colonial building of three rooms around a courtyard, refreshingly free from exuberant gilded decoration, which housed cases stuffed full of minerals from around the world. I was fascinated by the different coloured quartz, onyx, tourmalines, agates, sapphires; by the gold, copper and enormous chunks of semi-precious stones glinting with others buried inside. Completely ignorant, feet aching, I was intrigued by the bounty buried in the earth, compelled to write notes and to learn more.

By the time I limped out, bands were playing in every square, and heavy church doors had opened wide, revealing raucous Baroque interiors. Soft lights gleamed from larger houses, and an aura of gaiety and contentment seemed to permeate the little town.

Journal

Sat on a wall reading *Candide* by Voltaire, like a fairy tale but full of clichés. Then started Turgenev's *First Love*, in the bus station, but a boy peed all over the seat next to me, so I climbed up a steep hill with beautiful soft views over the town as the sun set pink behind. I'd been to the mining village of Mariana on overcrowded local buses where a small Black boy followed me around, opening doors, jabbering incessantly in this Portuguese which I don't understand. So many interesting faces I would like to draw, it seems a melting pot of different races, from the dark-skinned legacy of slavery to the paler bodies of those who once colonised the country.

Humidity is heavy and energy-sapping. Dragged myself to the synagogue to collect my bag and said goodbye to the swarm of men. I still don't know who they are, but their kindness is extraordinary. Now on another crowded bus heading back to Rio through the night, watching silhouettes of trees throwing down shadows in our path against the blackness of hills behind.

Waves pounded in on Ipanema and the misty days offered an unusual indifference between sea and sky, unlike the Rio in my head, and it slowly dawned on me that I had subconsciously and abruptly ended my travels. Even the tough city began to seem tame and too familiar. I needed to get my teeth into something more concrete than indulging my curiosity, and benefitting from the kindness of friends and strangers.

I explored the Enchanted Valley, a favela, or slum, of scrubby huts and no enchantment at all, searching for something, somewhere I could react to. I was drifting, perhaps saturated by so many months of absorbing new life, unable now to react with the same excitement and thrill of the new.

Sitting cross-legged on the white sands of Baja Beach, leaning against rocks, I read Kafka's *Metamorphosis*, and then moved on to *Zen and the Art of Motorcycle Maintenance* which went way over my head. I was distracted for a while as a man stood over me playing with himself, staring hard with wild eyes. Even he got bored and eventually wandered off, still fiddling furiously.

I didn't want to say goodbye to Ninian, to cut another cord, and feeling profoundly sad, I looked at all those unknown people around me, running, exercising, playing cards, old and young lying in heaps of colours and shapes, unselfconscious whatever their size. They could never be British. Lovers kissed, every bench occupied. Macumba pyres burnt, twinkling as dusk settled in around them.

My carefree existence had reached its final Latin American destination; the tattered air ticket was proffered, and a flight to London booked. Ninian tried hard to persuade me to stay, and it took a determination I didn't feel to stick with my plans. Each farewell felt like a kind of death, as I met friends to say goodbye, knowing I was unlikely to see most of them again. As if in a dream, I was about to step over another threshold towards a world in which, until now, I felt I had never belonged. No more evading a disintegrating family. Time was up, and I would forever cherish every single day of my wandering.

EPILOGUE

Blowin' In The Wind

My father never wrote to me while I was away, and on my return he had vanished, refusing to tell anyone where he was. He did eventually, evasively, get in touch, but was forever ashamed that my mother had left him. She married his best friend, and wondered how she would cope with her new surname: O'Cock.

My grandparents, and their London home, became an anchor for me. My grandfather, Henry Denham, continued writing: two autobiographies, updating his series of sea guides to the Mediterranean coasts, books that were translated into several languages, and remain collected today.

My grandmother painted beautifully for the rest of her life. She could be found on Greek islands, having jumped off their yacht, deciding to stay and paint for a few weeks. They led a comfortable, bohemian life untouched by the social mores of a system that might in those days have held them, remaining creative and curious until they died.

Garry and Beryl, whom I met at the bus stop in Guatemala, remain firm friends. They continued roaming the world – I stayed with them in Sydney – and as years went by they spent several Christmases with us, my husband and children, in Scotland. They now live on a houseboat in Vancouver.

Dolores in São Paulo took her own life a few years after I stayed with them, leaving four children and Alberto.

The Dibos family stayed in Peru in spite of political upheavals, their home always a welcome refuge for visitors.

Bruce Chatwin published his first book, *In Patagonia*, to huge international acclaim and became famous for his writing, for his unforgettable personality and peripatetic way of life. We remained in touch through letters and postcards until he died, much too young, at the age of forty-eight.

I also kept in touch with his cousins from Lima, the Barnetts, and with the clarity of time became fond of Monica.

Federico Gutierrez, with whom I spent Christmas in Salvador, came to England soon after my return and spent Christmas with my mother and new stepfather in their house, still being restored. I warned him there was little furniture and a lot of dust in a small village in the countryside, but he turned up in immaculate velvet suit and cloak, swept into the little local church on the green, waltzed up to the altar and curtsied low before turning with a flamboyant flourish to face a bemused tweed-clad congregation. When the service was over, we sat on straw bales in the back of a trailer, pulled by a stuttering skeletal tractor, singing carols around the village.

In those days, in the country, after dinner there was a convention where men often stayed in the dining room to drink port, while the women went upstairs to 'powder their noses'.

Federico sprinted out after the women, and lay on my mother's bed watching giggling, embarrassed English matrons utterly thrown by this breach of protocol. I suspect his Christmas was as memorable as mine had been, for very different reasons.

In Mexico, Patrick Tritton eventually remarried and had a happy rest of his short life.

My uncle John Denham, who had engineered the cargo boat to Mexico with his great shipping friend, bought large tracts of coastline in Costa Rica and founded a nature reserve to save the giant turtle. Pacuare is a huge success, still thriving today.

Ronnie Biggs, the Great Train Robber, eventually returned to England after thirty-five years on the run. *The Guardian* obituary (18th December 2013) details his extraordinary life and escapades, evading all attempts to bring him home.

In Chile, my friendship with Maria Luisa remains as strong and close as the days we shared a flat in Madrid, in spite of the geographical distance. We know each other's families, and have supported each other through different difficult times. Their ancient home in the vineyards was destroyed in a massive earthquake and, after many years, has been rebuilt.

Stephen, the heartthrob in Chile, married a beautiful local girl but died too young. I never saw him again.

Annette Corbett had a tumour on her brain and died shortly after my wonderful time with her family in Argentina.

Strangely, I never saw my host in Rio, Ninian, again.

The Danish nymphomaniac and her husband who were so kind and hospitable in Mexico City stayed several times on my return to London. She seduced a friend of mine who had called in for a drink, and got more than he bargained for.

I have been back to Mexico, to Ecuador, Chile, Bolivia and Argentina, bowled over by their grandeur and beauty. But there is nothing quite like the searing memories of being in a country for the very first time.

SPOTIFY PLAYLIST: *A LONG WAY SOUTH*/SARA STEWART

Sailing – Sutherland Brothers

Bridge Over Troubled Water – Simon & Garfunkel

Beautiful Noise – Neil Diamond

(Sittin' On) The Dock Of The Bay – Otis Redding

The Most Beautiful Girl – Charlie Rich

Your Song – Elton John

Happy Xmas (War Is Over) – John Lennon, Yoko Ono & The Plastic Ono Band and The Harlem Community Choir

Coming Around Again – Carly Simon

We Gotta Get Out Of This Place – The Animals

Forever Young – Bob Dylan

Tous Les Garçons Et Les Filles – Françoise Hardy

Morning Has Broken – Cat Stevens

Imagine – John Lennon

River Deep – Mountain High – Ike & Tina Turner

The First Time Ever I Saw Your Face – Roberta Flack

You Don't Have To Say You Love Me – Dusty Springfield

Have You Ever Seen The Rain – Creedence Clearwater Revival

The Girl From Ipanema – Stan Getz, João Gilberto, Astrud Gilberto and Antônio Carlos Jobim

La Bamba – Trini Lopez

Blowin' In The Wind – Stevie Wonder

ACKNOWLEDGEMENTS

My thanks go to Robert O'Byrne for persistently encouraging me to continue writing, and for castigating self-deprecation. To Alexander and Philippa for their patient tech help, to Tania and Zoe for their motivating support. To the team at Bradt Guides, who have guided me with enthusiasm, efficiency and humour, with special thanks to Anna Moores, who has held my hand every step of the way. To Ross Dickinson for his beady editing. To Barnaby Rogerson for his advice and endorsement. And to all those who were there in South America, and helped me on my way fifty years ago, many of whom are not mentioned in these salvaged memories, but they know who they are.